Southern Living® GARDEN G

Low Maintenance

Series Editor: Lois Trigg Chaplin

Text by Glenn Morris

Oxmoor
House®

W

Contents

Book Division of Southern Progress Corporation
P.O. Box 2463, Birmingham, Alabama 35201

Southern Living® is a federally registered
trademark of Southern Living, Inc.

Library of Congress Catalog Number: 96-67717
ISBN: 0-8487-2246-9
Manufactured in the United States of America
First Printing 1997

We're Here for You!
We at Oxmoor House are dedicated to serving you
with reliable information that expands your imagi-
nation and enriches your life. We welcome your
comments and suggestions. Please write us at:

Oxmoor House, Inc.
Editor, LOW MAINTENANCE Garden Guide
2100 Lakeshore Drive
Birmingham, AL 35209

Editor-in-Chief: Nancy Fitzpatrick Wyatt
Editorial Director, Special Interest Publications:
Ann H. Harvey
Senior Editor, Editorial Services: Olivia Kindig Wells
Art Director: James Boone

Southern Living Garden Guide
LOW MAINTENANCE

Series Editor: Lois Trigg Chaplin
Assistant Editor: Kelly Hooper Troiano
Copy Editor: Anne S. Dickson
Editorial Assistant: Laura A. Fredericks
Garden Editor, *Southern Living*: Linda C. Askey
Indexer: Katharine R. Wiencke
Concept Designer: Eleanor Cameron
Designer: Carol Loria
Senior Photographer, *Southern Living*: Van Chaplin
Production and Distribution Director: Phillip Lee
Associate Production Manager:
Vanessa Cobbs Richardson
Production Assistant: Valerie L. Heard

Our appreciation to the staff of *Southern Living*
magazine for their contributions to this book.

*L*ow-Maintenance *P*rimer 4

What Is Low-Maintenance
Landscaping? 6

Designing Your Landscape . . .12

Low-Maintenance Plantings . .20

Low-Maintenance
Lawn Design 26

Getting Started 32

The Basics of Care 39

Problems and Solutions 45

Special Gardens 54

Plant Hardiness Zone Map 62

Ginkgo tree

*P*lant *P*rofiles 63
Abelia 64
Aucuba 65
Azalea, Gumpo 66
Bald Cypress 67
Beech 68
Black-eyed Susan 69
Caladium 70
Canna 71
Chaste Tree 72
Cleyera 73
Coleus 74
Coneflower, Orange 75
Coneflower, Purple 76
Coreopsis 77
Cosmos 78
Crepe Myrtle 79
Daffodil 80
Daisy, Shasta 81
Daylily 82
Euonymus, Winged 83
Flowering Quince 84
Forsythia 85

Frontispiece: *selections of liriope*   Cover: *Japanese star jasmine,*
azaleas, tree-form privet

Ginkgo 86
Globe Amaranth 87
Goldenrain Tree 88
Hawthorn, Indian 89
Holly 90
Holly, Burford 92
Holly, Dwarf Yaupon 93
Holly, Yaupon 94
Hosta 95
Iris 96
Ivy, English 97
Leucothoe, Florida 98
Ligustrum 99
Liriope 100
Madagascar Periwinkle 101
Magnolia, Sweet Bay 102
Mahonia, Leatherleaf 103
Maple, Red 104
Maple, Sugar 105
Mondo Grass 106
Nandina 107
Oak, Live 108
Oleander 109
Pachysandra, Japanese 110
Pansy 111
Periwinkle 112
Pine, Loblolly 113
Pittosporum 114
Redbud 115
Rose-of-Sharon 116
Sedum 117
Spirea, Reeves 118
Star Jasmine, Japanese 119
Viburnum, Doublefile 120
Wax Begonia 121
Wax Myrtle 122
Zinnia, Narrowleaf 123
Pest and Disease Control 124
Index 126

Mondo grass

Low-Maintenance Primer

*Learn to take charge
of your garden without
it taking charge of you.*

Few activities are as satisfying as planting a garden and nurturing it. Not surprisingly, "diggin' in the dirt" scores high marks as a recreational activity. The reasons are several: there is no travel involved; it is not expensive, or at least you can control the cost; and, perhaps most important, gardening is productive and creative.

When you finish gardening for the day or even the hour, that corner of the world where you were working looks better than it did before you started. Or you walk away knowing that it is just a matter of time until it will be attractive.

All of this has universal appeal. The efforts of gardening have long been admired and even celebrated. Historic gardens, such as Biltmore House in Asheville, North Carolina, or Dumbarton Oaks in Washington, D.C., or Bok Tower Gardens in Lake Wales, Florida, are destinations in their own rights. Garden cities, among them Charleston and Savannah, draw tourists who want not only to sample the historical vistas but also to peek through the gates surrounding the artfully constructed gardens.

Even these grand and elaborate gardens were first and foremost useful spaces to those who created them. They suited their owners' lifestyle and were functional as well as pleasing.

Meeting the practical needs of the household for outside space comes first, but the fun part comes next: creating a setting of joy and delight. The love of gardening, of nurturing plants and arranging them into an ensemble that creates a setting of original beauty, still motivates us, especially on weekends. You may not have legions of gardeners working artfully crafted acres, but you still want a beautiful garden. The only thing missing today seems to be the time to garden.

Use masses of easy-care ground cover, such as liriope, to reduce maintenance.

A lawn will require less time to maintain when bordered by neat beds of shrubs and ground covers in the more difficult areas.

This book tells you how to maintain the grounds of your home in handsome fashion in minimal time, an approach commonly referred to as "low-maintenance landscaping." The goal of this approach is to be in charge of a good-looking garden without having it be in charge of you.

What Is Low-Maintenance Landscaping?

The low-maintenance approach to gardening strives to achieve maximum effect with minimum effort.

If you were to go to the nearest forest and step beneath the cover of the trees and look around, you would see a low-maintenance landscape. The same phrase would describe a fallow field slowly becoming overgrown or the tangle of a thicket crowding a stream bank. Each of these environments needs no human help to thrive.

For most suburban settings and the peace of mind of most homeowners, leaving nature alone to do the "landscaping" is a bit too wild, although it is certainly low maintenance. You probably will prefer to tinker with nature a bit, to tame it so that it will enhance both the house and the neighborhood. This requires maintenance. How much depends on what you want to do. A gardener who loves fussing over hybrid tea roses will not see them as a lot of work but rather a pleasure. Yet these plants require twenty times the work it takes to care for flowers such as black-eyed Susans or orange daylilies. However, it is a mistake for you to think that a low-maintenance landscape is a no-maintenance landscape.

Although a pool requires attention, you can surround its edge with low-maintenance perennials and shrubs for an easy-care landscape.

Ways To Reduce Maintenance

Experienced gardeners know that low-maintenance landscaping is an approach to gardening where you are constantly seeking ways to reduce the amount of work needed to keep a garden healthy and attractive. This approach is governed by whether or not a task will make long-term gardening easier or more difficult. If the task will not make it easier, or if the task is unnecessary, do not do it. The two basic things you can do to eliminate excess work are to simplify design and reduce repetitive tasks.

Simplify Design

Your garden design can help you work more efficiently. For example, the design of the lawn should make mowing as easy and quick as possible. You may wish to replace some lawn with ground cover beds and eliminate hard-to-mow edges. As you work in the garden, look for other ways to eliminate extra steps, such as the drudgery of drag-

This artfully designed entry deck bridges a wet spot in the lawn to create a dry walkway. Plants that thrive in a wet environment, such as river birch, take advantage of the conditions.

ging hoses to water remote plants. Take the time to install a spigot or an automatic irrigation system to make watering simpler. The easier garden tasks are to accomplish, the less burdensome they become.

Low-maintenance design will also solve problems. If you have a steep slope to mow, try blanketing it with a ground cover such as ivy. Sometimes you can create simple plantings or make structural changes in a landscape to correct maintenance problems, such as poor drainage and worn paths. (See pages 45–53 for more about specific design solutions.)

What Is Low-Maintenance Landscaping?

Select shrubs based on their mature size to prevent the recurring problem of plants outgrowing their setting.

Reduce Repetitive Garden Tasks

Once you have simplified your garden design, the next step is to minimize repetitive tasks and eliminate the annoying ones. If a shrub must be pruned repeatedly because it covers up a living room window, replace it with a shrub that will not grow that tall.

Certain gardening tasks, among them weeding, mowing, pruning, and watering, are jobs that must be repeated to maintain a landscape. Whenever possible, reduce the frequency of these tasks. For example, mulch shrub beds to reduce weeds as well as lessen the need for frequent watering. To reduce lawn mowing, probably the most repeated task in any landscape, mow at the proper height and water and fertilize only enough to keep the lawn healthy but not growing so vigorously that it requires extra mowing. You may also minimize

Substitute a grasslike ground cover, such as mondo grass, for a lawn to eliminate mowing.

the time you spend caring for a lawn by reducing its size. You can plant ground covers, create flower beds, or even increase the size of your walk or drive.

Natural Cycles in the Garden

Gardens are never static. In some manner, whether it be the size of plants, the color of their foliage, or the production of flowers and fruit, gardens are always changing. These changes and the natural cycles of the seasons dictate which maintenance tasks take priority.

Seasonal Tasks for Garden Maintenance

With a low-maintenance approach to gardening, you need to consider all the changes that occur in a garden throughout the year. The natural calendar cycle of plants—from winter dormancy through the growing seasons to leaf drop in the fall—controls the list of garden chores. Here are some of the basic tasks that cannot be ignored.

One of the first maintenance tasks of the new growing season is fertilizing.

Fertilizing. During spring, plants emerge from dormancy as the sun warms the soil and activates their roots. This is jump-start time for most plants, a time of high nutritional need, especially for lawn grasses, which respond very quickly to changing temperatures. Not surprisingly, one of the first annual garden chores is fertilizing.

Weeding. Spring and fall bring a new crop of weeds to bare soil and poorly kept lawns. An easy way to minimize the time you spend weeding a lawn is to apply a pre-emergence herbicide (or "weed preventer"), such as crabgrass preventer. You can save more time by purchasing a product that combines fertilizer and preventer in one bag so that you can spread both in a single application. You must apply a pre-emergence herbicide at the correct time, as it does not work on weed seeds that have already sprouted. For spring lawn weeds, you should apply in early spring. For fall weeds, apply in late August (or no later than Labor Day) in the South.

You can set out container-grown plants any time of the year, but fall is usually best. In most areas of the South, the ground stays warm enough in fall for roots to grow while the top of the plant is dormant.

Mulching. Mulching suppresses weeds and reduces the need for frequent watering during drought. Replenishing mulch is also one of the best and easiest ways to dress up a planting bed. In winter, this additional protection further insulates the roots of more tender plants to help them survive freezing temperatures. And a late fall or early winter mulch neatens the appearance of the garden.

Planting. If you plant trees and shrubs at the proper time, they will not need the extra watering required of those planted during the growing season. Planting dates vary from region to region. Spring calls for the planting of summer bedding plants, while fall is a good time to plant most perennials, trees, and shrubs in the South. In fall, the plant's top is dormant and places no demands on the root system for food and water. The soil is still warm so that new roots can develop on the plants. When spring arrives, these plants will be better able to support new growth and make it through the summer.

Seasonal Shifts in Garden Maintenance

As the seasons change, so does the nature of garden maintenance. Both the type of work and the intensity of the task vary throughout the year. Understanding these natural shifts will help you know what to expect and to plan accordingly for long-term maintenance. If spring is the busiest time of year for you, design a landscape that makes minimal demands at that time. Here are some examples of common maintenance chores that each season will require.

Spring brings frequent mowing. In areas where cool-season grasses are predominant, the fertilizer spreader and the lawn mower are the first tools out of the garden shed. Cool-season grasses, such as fescue and bluegrass, surge in late winter through spring, rest during summer, and then thrive again as the weather cools in fall. Growth is rapid, making it difficult to maintain the grass at a neatly clipped height with just one weekly mowing. Warm-season grasses, such as Bermuda and centipede, surge in late spring and go dormant with the first frost in fall.

Summer brings watering, weeding, and more mowing. Watering is the most critical garden task during the summer months. Cool-season grasses tend to go dormant as heat increases, so you must water regularly to keep your lawn green. Warm-season grasses need regular watering and extra water during prolonged drought. In fact, all landscape plants need water during extended hot, dry weather. In addition, you will need to weed and mow more frequently as the warm weather encourages a big crop of weeds, such as crabgrass in the lawn and flower beds. You can reduce the amount of time you spend watering and weeding by using plants that are most tolerant of heat and drought.

Fall brings raking and cutting back. Fall is the season to clean up fallen leaves and summer bedding plants and perennials browned by frost. It is the ideal time to minimize next year's maintenance by transplanting ill-placed plants, planting ground covers that reduce the size of the lawn, and planting container-grown plants. This is also the time to prune troublesome branches and reshape plants to better direct next year's growth.

View fallen leaves and pine needles as a gift rather than a bother. The best way to improve your soil is to allow fallen vegetation to decay. Structuring your garden so that leaves fall where they can be chopped with a mower and used as mulch is one way of making leaf removal easier. Or let fallen leaves remain on the ground in woodland areas.

Winter brings structural changes. In winter, the garden lies dormant, affording the gardener a break from physical labor. This is a good time to decide what possible design changes need to be made. You may even want to work with a garden designer and horticulturist in winter. In spring, they will be busy and in high demand. Even if the changes cannot be implemented in the dead of winter, you will be first on the list when the weather is right.

CHANGES AS PLANTS GROW

As a gardener, you must reckon with the inevitable changes that occur in the garden as plants grow. For example, a sunny garden can become a shady one as trees grow. This affects the suitability and performance of the original plantings, which may not do well in shade. Changes of this nature happen gradually, but you can prevent future problems by making well thought-out plant choices when you plan your garden.

Pine needles are nature's gift. With this lawn configuration, it is easy to rake the needles to an adjacent bed, where they serve as mulch.

Designing Your Landscape

The first step in designing an easy-care landscape is to consider the physical features of the site.

Every lot is bound by features that influence how a landscape is designed. Long-term maintenance begins early with decisions about how to address existing factors such as the slope and other physical features of the site. You will also need to consider how rainfall and sunlight affect your landscape as well as the style of garden and plants you want to include. This is true whether you want to reduce maintenance of an existing landscape or plan a new landscape around your home.

Physical Features of the Site

First you need to consider such physical features of the site as lot alignment, slope, soil, and existing trees. Some of these, such as the direction the house faces, cannot be changed. Likewise, a steep slope, poor drainage, or the existing tree cover may be too expensive or time consuming to change. A low-maintenance landscape tries to use what nature gives it. The better you can adapt your garden design to the existing features of the site, the more successful your low-maintenance effort will be.

Before: *This lot was a maintenance nightmare with a difficult slope and shrubs that were ill suited to their location.*

After: *The owners tamed the slope with a little grading and chose proper plants for the site. A grouping of dogwood trees, azaleas, and yew greets guests at the front door.*

Site Topography and Alignment

The *topography* of a site refers to any change in elevation. Steeply sloping sites present a greater challenge because they are difficult to maneuver and dangerous or impossible to mow. It is always less expensive or less arduous to plant a slope with a durable ground cover, such as ivy, than to create level ground by using a retaining wall or bringing in earth. However, you may need retaining walls on a steep slope to make adequate room for the plantings you wish to have on the site.

Flat sites present few maintenance problems. One exception is when the soil on a flat site does not drain after a rainfall or when water flows down to the site.

The *alignment,* or the compass direction that any slope of the land faces, has a direct impact on garden maintenance. Alignment affects the temperature of the site and how well plants do at any given point on the site.

The north-facing part of the property tends to be the coolest since the sun's rays strike at a more oblique angle. Lots exposed to the east have the most favorable conditions for growing—a good exposure to morning sun but little or no exposure to searing afternoon rays. South-facing lots will bear the brunt of the most direct sun. These lots have a milder exposure in winter but are subject to maximum drying and heat stress produced by the summer sun.

The hottest section of a site is usually on the southwest side. Plants on this side of a building, wall, or large rock formation are especially hard hit. In these locations, the severest rays of the sun strike the structure directly and reflect onto the ground, making the soil temperature much hotter. Such a spot could be a full USDA Zone hotter than the average annual summer temperature of the region.

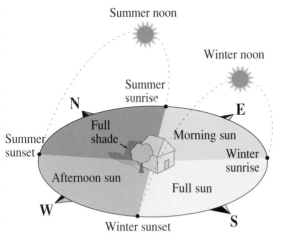

Sun Alignment Diagram

Existing Trees

Existing trees, particularly large shade trees, are one of the greatest assets of a site. Large trees shelter a site, creating shade and cool temperatures. Unfortunately, they also shade lawns and compete with grass for nutrients. You may prune or thin dense trees to let through more light. You can also reduce some of the maintenance large trees require, especially in fall, by making a bed of mulch or ground cover beneath the canopy. Many trees also drop nuts or seedpods as well as leaves, adding to seasonal cleanup chores. You may have to weed the seedlings in the spring or rake leaves that do not fall through the ground cover.

Work with existing trees to reap the reward of a beautiful garden planting that requires no extra maintenance.

Soil

Rich soil grows healthier plants that are better able to withstand drought, disease, and insect damage. By modifying or improving the poor soil common to most sites, you can help reduce long-term maintenance. Although soil modification requires extra work and money, over the long run, it is well worth the expense.

Soil made of heavy clay is difficult for roots to penetrate. It often traps water, creating drainage problems. If you are able to roll a "clay snake" with a handful of soil, you need to work organic matter, such as peat moss, well-rotted manure or sawdust, or pulverized pine bark, into the soil to reduce the heaviness.

If you have sandy soil, which drains too well, you can add peat moss or well-rotted manure (or other organic matter) to increase the soil's ability to hold water and nutrients.

After working amendments into the soil, have the soil tested for pH and nutrient content. This information will help you select fertilizers. It will also let you know how much lime to add if the soil is too acidic. (See page 33 for more about soil testing.)

Sunlight

The hours of sunlight determine what you should plant at any location. You may observe plants in your garden growing weak from lack of light or plants that are sunburned or stunted from too much sun. To avoid maintenance problems, match plants to a site appropriate to their needs. Sunlight is a critical factor. For example, some plants, such as azaleas, will grow in sun or shade. However, because they attract more pests in sun, it is a good idea to grow them in shade to reduce maintenance.

When choosing plants, be aware of how the sun strikes all areas of your property. Full sun is generally considered to be six hours of uninterrupted sunlight between 9:00 a.m. and 4:00 p.m. Lawn grasses require a minimum of four to five hours of direct sunlight to do their best. Use areas with less sunlight for plants suited to partial shade.

Experienced gardeners know that the specific time the sun shines on a site will also make a difference. Early-morning sun (until 10:30 a.m.) provides sufficient light for growth and flowers but without damaging intensity. You should consider midday summer sun (11:00 a.m. to 3:00 p.m.) and late afternoon sun (from 2:30 p.m. until sunset) as full sun as far as plant selection is concerned.

Shade-tolerant caladiums brighten the path leading to this entrance.

Rainfall

Select plants, especially lawn grasses, that will thrive with the average rainfall cycles of your area to reduce maintenance. Extended annual drought, for example, is common in the Southwest. Locally adapted plants, such as buffalo grass, have a track record for surviving such conditions without extra watering.

For best results, look to plants such as wax myrtle that are able to thrive with average swings in rainfall. See that they are deeply rooted in well-prepared beds; then ensure that they can survive drought with minimal attention by heavily mulching them. This will reduce the moisture loss through evaporation.

Garden Design

Garden design is the art of arranging the landscape so that it fits your lifestyle and is attractive. Regardless of the style you choose, your garden should not require a week of Sundays to maintain, unless you love gardening and want to be outside all week.

Good garden design relies on repeated shapes, forms, and plants. How you go about achieving these patterns can make the difference between a garden that demands a lot of maintenance and one

This backyard design creates large sweeping beds with a limited number of easy-care plants. The main chores are mowing and occasional edging, mulching, and gathering leaves.

A simple brick path also serves as an edging that separates the lawn and holly ferns from a larger woodland area.

that requires minimal work. While there are ways to reduce maintenance tasks in all gardens, you should not plan an elaborate landscape if your schedule keeps you from maintaining it.

Simple Designs

The simpler the garden, the easier the maintenance. A garden that is composed of many features scattered across the site will increase your maintenance time. Complicated patterns of lawns and beds require well-defined edges to look good, and maintaining these edges takes time.

On the other hand, larger but fewer beds with masses of a minimal number of plants are easier to maintain. For the focus of your garden, choose a dominant shape or feature—an easily mowed lawn, a mulched planting bed, a ground cover bed, or a gazebo. This focal point will give a simple garden greater visual impact and minimizes your maintenance efforts.

Formal and Informal Gardens

Formal gardens can be tedious and time consuming if you must trim shrubs to a preferred shape or size. However, a formal garden that depends on walls, paths, or paving for its formal effect and has only a small shaped lawn as its centerpiece can be a low-maintenance landscape. A formal garden will adapt better to sites with little or no slope and uniform growing conditions throughout.

Typically, an informal or natural garden does not have a preconceived pattern but instead is arranged according to how you use the garden and the site's physical features. This flexibility makes it possible for you to "work around" difficult portions of the site with an eye to minimizing long-term maintenance. This gives informal gardens an advantage in low-maintenance design because their loose organization makes them suitable for difficult terrain and challenging site conditions. In an informal garden, you have more freedom to adapt your plantings to the site; in a formal garden, you impose a structured garden plan upon it.

Special Features

Special features, such as shrub borders, fountains, and walkways, add interest to a garden. All of these, however, will not be appropriate for a low-maintenance landscape, so it is advisable to know what to expect before deciding on a particular garden treatment.

Features That Create Special Demands

The following garden features will require special maintenance demands during the gardening year. While the demands are not extraordinary, the time adds up if you have set your sights on having many of these features (or a lot of one kind) in your garden. Think of these higher maintenance items as "what-not-to-do" unless you are able to spend the extra time they require. In a low-maintenance garden, you will want to limit the following to those you simply cannot live without.

Lightweight vines, such as clematis, bring color into a garden but will not tear up the latticework.

Water features. Water features, such as fountains and pools, require diligent cleaning of algae, fallen leaves, and other natural debris. You must clean any pumps or recirculation systems, and you may need to drain shallow pools and shut down fountains in winter.

Pruned shrubs. Artificially shaped shrubs require a great deal of maintenance. Repeated shearing takes time. Shearing also distorts the growth of the plant, eventually inhibiting the type of growth needed to sustain the crisp original sheared form. You may have to replace mature sheared shrubs or rejuvenate them by drastic, unsightly pruning. If you must have a pruned hedge, choose a small-leafed, slow-growing plant with a mature height and shape similar to the formal hedge you want to create. If a 3-foot clipped hedge is what you need, you may want to try a dwarf yaupon.

Bark, gravel, and dirt walkways. While bark, gravel, and dirt walking surfaces are pleasant to tread, these surfaces present high-maintenance demands. All of them must have a containing edge, and heavy rainfall can wash them away. Leaf removal can be difficult, weeds can grow in them, and annual replenishment is usually required.

Garden structures. You must maintain any wooden outdoor structure, such as a trellis, arbor, fence, or outbuilding, against the damaging effects of moisture, sun, and insects. Latticework may pull apart, so use it only for growing lightweight vines. If a structure is painted, it will require a new coat of paint every few years. Up-front protective measures, such as using rot-resistant materials, are expensive but save money in the long run.

Mixed flowers, such as this bed of black-eyed Susan, Madagascar periwinkle, and narrow-leaf zinnia, demand seasonal attention. Make it low maintenance by limiting the size of the bed.

DEADHEADING

Deadheading, or removing spent blossoms, will keep some species of annuals and perennials blooming longer. When you remove the old flowers as they fade, you keep the plant from forming seed and cause it to make more flowers. A few easy-care annuals that respond well to this procedure are cosmos, branching sunflowers, and pansies. Perennials that will need deadheading include coreopsis, gaillardia, and reblooming daylilies, such as Stella de Oro.

One particular garden annoyance is weedy growth at the base of posts. When these posts are surrounded by lawn, you must trim the grass at their base by hand or with a string trimmer, which creates an additional chore.

Mixed flower borders. A border of mixed annuals and perennials can be a joy to look at, but it will need seasonal maintenance. These plantings require weeding, mulching, fertilizing, watering, pruning, dividing, deadheading, and transplanting. Some may have to be staked.

Hanging baskets and containers. Plants in baskets and containers will need more water in the summer. The larger the container, the longer it takes to dry out, so choose large pots and restrict the number of them if you wish to reduce maintenance.

Low-Maintenance Features

Some garden features that look time consuming are actually low-maintenance options. Many of these fulfill a pressing need but do not demand much work. When properly integrated, the features below can work together to create a neat, attractive, low-maintenance landscape design.

Genuine natural areas. Many large lots include wooded areas that may, for the most part, be left alone. Sometimes these areas will require annual clearing of vines, honeysuckle, or sprouting privet, but overall, a natural woodland requires less maintenance than a cultivated landscape. A natural area may take the form of an island in a large yard. A woodland between your house and a neighbor's can serve as a screen. You can enjoy these areas more by creating a garden getaway with a bench, grill, or gazebo at the edge of the woods.

Mixed shrub borders. For little maintenance, try plantings of mixed shrubs, such as aucuba and leucothoe, under trees, or forsythia and spirea along the border of the lawn. Match the plants to the setting and size requirements, plant well, mulch thoroughly, water as needed, and enjoy the show.

Properly placed native plants. Plant a healthy native plant in conditions that match its natural habitat to eliminate some garden woes. Native plants tend to tolerate the natural conditions of an area, such as soils that are wet, dry, or alkaline. However, do not exclude good plants if they are not native. Try driving through old neighborhoods to get ideas for tried-and-true plants for an area, both native and exotic.

Established ground cover beds. An ideal ground cover plant supports vigorous growth and is known for its durability. Ground covers leave you less lawn to mow and solve many problems, from what to plant under the shade of a large tree to how to cover a steep slope. However, establishing a bed of ground cover will require considerable work at first. You will need to water, fertilize, and pull weeds until the planting fills out.

Concrete or brick surfaces and paved walks. Pavement requires very little maintenance. Just be sure that rainfall will drain off, that there are expansion joints to prevent cracking, and that any lawn next to it can be mowed completely, without trimming. Remember that in time, large trees planted too close to a paved surface will lift or crack the surface.

Properly established lawns. A lawn, or at least a grassy area, is a must for some households. A well-established, healthy lawn requires weekly mowing and watering during its growing season. In very hot weather or drought, it is best to delay mowing and water infrequently but thoroughly. If maintenance is a problem, reduce the size of the lawn.

This mass of liriope covers surface roots that make mowing difficult.

If you have a well-established lawn of manageable size, proper mowing is the key to keeping it attractive.

Low-Maintenance Plantings

Choose plants that are compatible with the conditions in your garden.

The low-maintenance approach to gardening strives to develop a landscape that is as self-sufficient as possible. Much of this approach is simple common sense, but the irony is that you must know something about gardening to recognize what can be done easily or should not be done at all. Here are some of the things you need to consider when planning a garden that will take care of itself most of the time.

Avoid Mistakes in Plant Selection

Choosing plants that are suited to conditions in your garden is crucial to lowering maintenance. The ideal plant is one that performs whatever function is necessary yet requires little or no pruning and only occasional watering and feeding to thrive. If you select plants wisely, you will not have to coax growth or worry about pests, diseases, and the plant's health. Here are some plant types you will want to avoid because of the maintenance problems they create.

Marginally Suited Plants

Plants that are on the fringes of their hardiness zone invite trouble. Extreme winter or summer temperatures can cause severe dieback or kill plants that have been forced into growing at the edge of their recommended hardiness range. If extreme temperature does not kill them outright, repeated seasonal stress will stunt growth and may increase the plants' susceptibility to disease. In the South, heat tolerance is as important as winter hardiness; many plants such as hemlocks or white pines that do well in the Appalachian Mountains will struggle in the warmer climate of the Piedmont area.

Plants set in the wrong place—shade-loving plants in full sun, for example—will be stressed and susceptible to insect infestation or disease. Conversely, sun-loving plants deprived of sun will have spindly growth, sparser foliage, and fewer flowers.

Native ferns flourish as an ornamental ground cover in this moist, shady location that is similar to their natural environment.

Troublesome Plants

Some plants have natural characteristics that may make them seem like a good idea when you plant them. However, traits such as dropping limbs, undesirable fruit, invasive root systems, and vigorously spreading growth habits may eventually place them on the high-maintenance list.

Check with your local nursery about the downside of a particular plant, and then evaluate the maintenance load it brings to the garden. You may be able to manage the burden in a less time-consuming way. Sweetgum is a superb, disease-resistant, fast-growing shade tree that tolerates poor soil, but it is notorious for its annual dropping of "gumballs." To avoid the problem, plant it in a mulched area, or choose the fruitless cultivar Rotundiloba.

Fast-Growing Plants

Do not be tempted by fast-growing plants, such as Lombardy poplar or silver maple, that are touted as quick screens or instant shade. Large shrubs and trees that grow exceptionally fast may fill a garden need for a short time, but they are usually structurally weak and subject to devastation by wind, snow, or ice. Also, a fast-growing plant, such as fiercely invasive bamboo, may quickly outgrow its location to become an annual pruning chore.

Plant Borders for Your Advantage

A bed or a border is a defined area in your garden that contains trees, shrubs, and flowering plants. You can enjoy the seasonal beauty of a garden by planting spring-flowering trees or summer-flowering perennials in borders. You simply need to plan carefully and select plants that will ensure interesting borders and that require attention only a few times a year.

Decide on Formal or Informal

Low-maintenance borders may be geometrical shapes filled with carefully placed plantings or free-flowing shapes created by a casual grouping of plants. Personal preference generally influences the shape of a border, though free-form beds tend to be less demanding. There is a higher visual premium on uniformity in a formal garden, which sometimes requires pruning or other maintenance to keep it neat. Informal low-maintenance plantings often have a greater variety of plants, which will create a more diverse look.

Compatible plants keep these free-flowing borders of mixed trees, shrubs, and flowers low maintenance.

21

A Place for Leaves

Borders under existing trees provide a logical place in which to rake leaves that fall. They are a low-maintenance solution to an annual garden chore.

Decaying leaves are nature's original source of organic matter, and raking them into a border only makes for better growing conditions for shade-loving shrubs. The leaves decay to become mulch that helps sustain the shrubs through future droughts. They also serve as a source of nutrients. Mow the leaves before distributing them to reduce their bulk and hasten decay.

Group Plants That Require Similar Conditions

One way to ensure that a border does not require extra work is to group plants that thrive in similar conditions. This will simplify your work load because all the plants in the border have like requirements for moisture, soil type, and sun.

For sunny sites, rely entirely on sun-loving plants, such as forsythia, bridalwreath spirea, or barberry. To avoid a potential maintenance headache, do not mix shade-loving azaleas into such a planting. In the sun, azaleas are prone to heat stress and infestations of lacebugs.

Other things to consider when mixing like plants are their need for water and their tolerance of heavy soil. You do not want to plant a rhododendron, which will quickly become diseased in heavy wet clay, next to ginger lilies or another plant that you would have to water frequently during the summer.

Try Mixed Borders

Planting a combination of trees, shrubs, annuals, and perennials in a single border brings seasonal effects in different heights and at different times of the year. Again, the key is to select plants that do not spread out of control and that thrive in similar horticultural conditions so that only general, not specialized, maintenance is necessary. Variety in a border not only makes it more interesting, but it also minimizes the risk of complete devastation from extreme conditions, such as drought or severe cold. However, remember that the greater the variety, the more varied the maintenance needs. If your mixed border contains more than a few types of plants, you may spend more time pruning, dividing, and deadheading.

Space Plants Properly

Proper spacing is another step toward the long-term health and lower maintenance of a border. Be sure to give young plants plenty of room to grow. They may look lonely at first, but this practice will go a long way toward ensuring a healthy plant. Crowding plants invites diseases and may create a need for earlier pruning. In the first few years while border plantings fill in, place annuals and perennials between the plants to give the border a more finished look.

Space plants used in borders, such as these azaleas, far enough apart to fill in but not outgrow their location.

Use Ground Covers

A ground cover can be any plant that is used to cover large areas of a garden instead of a lawn grass. Typically, these plants are hardy and inexpensive and, once established, require little maintenance. Ground covers can be vines, such as ivy, or they may spread underground, such as pachysandra. Even low-growing shrubs, such as dwarf barberry or dwarf quince, can be planted in a mass as ground cover.

What Ground Covers Do

Ground covers bring a sweep of texture to the garden and help unify sections of the landscape. At the same time, they can greatly reduce garden maintenance by covering the ground with a single plant species that only needs attention once or twice a year. Masses of ground cover can dramatically cut the time you spend mowing your lawn.

Delineate the lawn. Ground covers are very useful for giving shape to the lawn by providing contrasting texture and color in the garden. They also solve problems in areas of the garden where the grass struggles due to too much shade or competition with tree roots. In areas where they are hardy, a bed of common periwinkle, Japanese star jasmine, or English ivy is an excellent solution for covering troublesome areas.

Tie separate plants together. Ground covers can unite individual plantings into a single group by connecting free-standing specimens. They also eliminate mowing around individual plants. A good example of this appears on the cover of this book. This photograph shows a large sweep of Japanese star jasmine that links trees and shrubs, both large and small, that are dotted across a planting.

BEWARE OF COMMON BERMUDA

Common Bermuda is an invasive lawn grass that can turn a bed of ground cover into a weedy nightmare. Common Bermuda spreads into ground cover beds, rooting as it grows. Then it sends up shoots that hover above the bed like antennae. You can ensure a successful ground cover under these circumstances through vigilant edging and by planting dense dwarf shrubs.

If you have common Bermuda, it is best to avoid either making a mulched flower bed or planting ground covers, such as juniper, that cannot compete. (For more about Bermuda grasses, see page 30.)

This ivy ground cover defines the shape of the lawn and thrives where lawn grasses would struggle. The effect is a graceful, groomed, informal entrance.

Mulch as a Ground Cover

Occasionally, gardeners will depart from using a plant as a ground cover and use a mulch instead. Large islands of leaves, pine straw, or bark mulch often work well under dense trees where it can be difficult to grow plants. Of course, this is best on a site that is flat or gently sloping so that the rain does not wash away the mulch. To maintain the mulch, you only have to weed any sprouts that peek through and refresh the cover as it breaks down. To keep down weeds, the ground cover should be about 3 inches deep. Leaves that fall to the ground may be left where they are, but they can look messy (especially large leaves). Gather large leaves for composting, or run over piles of them with the lawn mower and then return the chopped leaves to the bed of mulch. Or wait until all the leaves have fallen and then cover them up with a layer of chopped leaves or pine straw.

Plan Flower Beds Wisely

A low-maintenance landscape can include the bright show of annual and perennial flowers. You will simply need to choose pest-free species that have a long life span, that are not invasive, and that do not need frequent dividing. Long-lived species that are easy to care for include daffodils, Siberian iris, peonies, daylilies, purple coneflowers, and yellow coneflowers. The following points will help you choose suitable flowers and place them wisely.

Concentrate Color To Reduce Maintenance

A few carefully placed flower beds can highlight a garden without becoming a maintenance nightmare. Establish flower beds in key locations where they produce the most impact. This is usually a place where you want people to look, such as the junction of the front walk and the driveway, where the beds can be a cheerful greeting; beside the front stoop; or next to garden features, such as statuary or a birdbath.

When selecting these locations, remember that the bed will be easier to manage if all parts receive the same amount of sunlight and have the same soil conditions.

Include Flowers That Bloom a Long Time

Choose flowers that bloom for many weeks or months over flowers with shorter blooming periods. You will find a balance between annuals and perennials, as each has a low-maintenance advantage.

Place bright long-lasting color in a few strategic places. This small bed of Melampodium combines high visual impact with low maintenance.

Annuals, the best of which often bloom for six months, generally are showier for a longer period than are perennials, which may bloom for three to six weeks. However, you must plant annuals every year.

Even the longest-blooming perennials, which can live for many years, rarely bloom as long as annuals. But the advantage of perennials is that you do not need to replant them each year. Perennials should be cut back after their tops die (usually in winter), and most must be divided every two or three years. Long-lived species that bloom for six weeks or more include cannas, many salvias, Shasta daisy, reblooming daylilies, Autumn Joy sedum, and ornamental grasses.

Plants with interesting foliage, such as coleus (an annual), ornamental grasses, hostas, and hardy ferns (all perennials), are ideal choices for long-lasting show in low-maintenance flower beds.

Avoid Flowers That Demand Special Attention

To reduce maintenance, avoid flowers that need staking or other extra care. Tall species, such as delphinium, foxglove, and dahlia, are easily beaten down by a heavy rain unless each of their stems is tied to a stake. However, some tall flowers have extra-sturdy stems that are more resistant. These include sunflowers and cannas.

This floral bonanza of impatiens and wax begonias will last from spring until frost.

Low-Maintenance Lawn Design

A clearly delineated lawn can become as important a part of the overall landscape design as the trees, shrubs, and flowers.

For lower maintenance, give your lawn a definite shape and reduce it to a manageable size.

Lawns are the most popular treatment of landscape space because they are an economical and easy means of covering a large area. They can also become a comfortable, practical space for outdoor living. However, lawns create a weekly mowing chore during the growing season, thus increasing maintenance.

Design Influences Maintenance

Aesthetically, lawns are the largest expanse of color and texture in most gardens, making them the unifying visual element in the landscape design. Keeping your lawn in good condition takes time, for you will need to mow, water, feed, weed, edge, thatch, and reseed. The secret of a low-maintenance lawn is to make it no larger than what you can easily keep healthy and vigorous.

Give the Lawn Sun

In any landscape design, the lawn should receive at least six to eight hours of sun each day. Lawns need full sun to grow thick and be able to compete with weeds. The more shade a lawn gets, the more work you will have to do to keep it attractive. When developing a landscape design, reserve the sunniest area for grass, and plant ground cover or borders in less sunny areas. Deep shade and root competition from large trees can make it impossible to grow grass. If you must have a lawn where such conditions exist, choose a grass that tolerates shade well. Tall fescue and cool-season blends selected for shade tolerance are the preferred cool-season grasses. Of the warm-season grasses, certain hybrids of St. Augustine are the best for the low-light areas.

Provide a Shape to the Lawn

All too often our only concept of a lawn is a sea of grass that extends across the property to the neighbor's lot line. However, lawns with a distinct outline, even if they are free flowing and informal, will contribute more to the overall look of your landscape and will usually be easier to maintain. If you give your lawn a shape defined by beds, borders, walkways, and other landscape features, the lawn itself will become a feature of the garden.

The exact shape of a lawn depends on such elements as the location of existing trees, the topography of the lot, the architectural style of the house, and your personal preference. Free-form shapes seem better adaptations for sites with steep terrain or with many existing trees. Open, flat sites, on the other hand, present few maintenance limitations, and the lawn shape may draw more directly from house architecture and personal preference.

Keep in mind that lawns in regular, compact shapes, such as circles or squares, are easier to mow and are usually less trouble to water and fertilize. In addition, such lawns have smaller perimeters than do free-form curvilinear lawns, thus reducing the time you spend edging or trimming. Small lawns surrounded by borders or beds of ground covers become like a rug in the landscape.

SLOPING GROUND

Lawns on sloping ground can be difficult and even unsafe to cut. A slope that is awkward to walk across will be even more awkward to mow. In fact, any ground with a slope exceeding 1 vertical foot for every 4 to 5 feet of horizontal length is hazardous and should not be considered for lawn. (See page 46 for more about slopes.)

This circular lawn is easy to water, and the brick edging makes it easy to mow.

Want to save time mowing? Change the corners of your lawn! Tight corners will have you backtracking to maneuver the mower into these wayward places. The solution is to round off the awkward spot.

Use a garden hose to lay out a pleasing alternative edge. Then push the mower beside the hose to see if the new edge is easy to follow. If it is, cut in the new shape and cut out the wasted time.

You might want to redesign the perimeter of the lawn to eliminate any spots that a mower cannot pass over smoothly in one easy swath.

Get rid of any lawn shapes that are narrower than your mower's cutting diameter.

Pick the Appropriate Size

The time you have to maintain a lawn should influence its size. While lawns do require care, they are highly demanding only part of the year. In fact, you will find that feeding, edging, trimming, and thatching your lawn are unnecessary in winter. But mowing and watering will consume your time during the growing season.

Look at the maximum amount of time you have available for lawn care per week, and then look at what the lawn needs in its most demanding season. (Remember that cool-season grasses take more time in spring and fall; warm-season grasses are most demanding in spring and summer.)

Then ask yourself these questions: Does the lawn design make weekly care efficient and easy? Do I have the time to water and mow properly? If your answers are no, then downsizing may be in order.

Choose the Right Lawn Grass

Proper grass selection is key to establishing a low-maintenance lawn. A locally adapted grass will better resist local weather extremes and prevalent diseases and pests than will a marginally suited grass. In addition, it is difficult for opportunistic weeds to succeed in a lawn that is thriving. Grass types that are inappropriate for a region will require extra work to keep the lawn healthy.

Lawn grasses are divided into two groups: *warm-season grasses* and *cool-season grasses.* Warm-season grasses grow fast in hot weather and go dormant, turning brown, when it is cold. Cool-season grasses behave the opposite; after surging in the spring, their growth slows considerably in the hot summer sun, and the grass may thin out or become worn looking during hot, dry weather, only to start growing rapidly again in the fall.

Warm-season grasses are successful from the southern part of Zone 7 south to the Atlantic Ocean and the Gulf of Mexico. A line connecting the cities of Norfolk, Raleigh, Greenville, Atlanta, Birmingham, Jackson, and Little Rock approximates the northern limit of the range. Refer to the chart on pages 30 and 31 for information on the recommended grasses. Zone 7 and the warmer parts of Zone 6 are generally known as the transition zone. In nearly all of this area, you can grow either the most cold tolerant of the warm-season grasses, such as Zoysia, or the most heat tolerant of the cool-season grasses, such as tall fescue. Mixes of fescue, bluegrass, and perennial ryegrass are popular, but only the tall fescue is likely to fare well in heat.

GRASS MIXES

Unlike warm-season grasses, you can mix cool-season grasses to create a very uniform lawn. Often several species, such as Kentucky bluegrass, tall fescue, and perennial ryegrass, are combined in a seed mix. This mix helps create a low-maintenance lawn because it combines the strengths of all the species. Mixes are often the best choice for low-maintenance turf in regions where cool-season grasses grow best.

Also, by using a mix, you get adaptability with a single feeding for various growing conditions—creeping red fescue succeeds in shade while tall fescue dominates in sun.

The strawlike color of Zoysia in dormancy is a feature of the winter landscape.

WARM-SEASON GRASSES

Bahia. Bahia is a coarse-textured lawn grass that will grow in poor, sandy soil, making it ideal for the coastal South. It has few pests and grows easily from seed. Fertilizing needs are minimal, but mowing must be done frequently because the grass has foot-tall seed heads.

Bermuda. Among the warm-season grasses, common Bermuda may be the most widely grown. It is exceptionally drought tolerant and quick to establish, forming a solid lawn from seed in just one year. It also tolerates salt spray and is tough enough to use for athletic fields, making it ideal for high-traffic locations. However, it is not very cold hardy and will not tolerate even light shade. In sun, Bermuda is very aggressive and, in fact, will invade and take over ground cover and flower beds.

Improved Bermuda selections, such as Texturf, Tifgreen, Tifway, Tifway II, and Tufcoat, have better color but higher fertilizing, mowing, and watering needs.

Buffalo grass. Buffalo grass is a native prairie grass that is a success as a lawn grass in the drought-prone areas of the Southwest. It is durable and has low fertilizing requirements. New selections, such as Prairie, form a thick turf.

Centipede. Centipede is an ideal choice for the lower South because it will grow in both highly acidic and poor soils. It requires only one feeding a year—too much fertilizer will kill it—and a little iron-rich supplement to help maintain a deep green color.

St. Augustine. St. Augustine is a rapidly spreading grass with wide, stout blades that give it a coarse texture. The grass is salt tolerant and light-shade tolerant, making it popular along the Gulf and South Atlantic coasts. The selection Raleigh will hold its green color long after other warm-season grasses have turned brown.

Zoysia. Zoysia is the South's most refined grass, one that creates a soft, lush, thick carpet. Healthy stands can choke out weeds, are drought tolerant, and will grow in light shade. This fine-textured grass is usually sold only as sod and is slow (and expensive) to establish but, once in place, it is worth the wait. Emerald and Myers are the two most popular selections.

RECOMMENDED GRASSES FOR THE SOUTH

Grass	Zones
Bahia	8, 9
Bermuda, common	7, 8, 9
Bermuda, improved	7, 8, 9
Buffalo grass	8, 9
Centipede	8, 9
Kentucky bluegrass	6, 7
Perennial ryegrass	6, 7
St. Augustine	8, 9
Tall fescue	6, 7, 8
Zoysia	7, 8, 9

Texture	Drought Resistance	Shade Tolerance	Fertilizer Needs	Method of Establishment
Coarse	Excellent	Poor	Low	Seed
Medium	Excellent	Poor	Moderate	Seed, plugs, sprigs, sod
Medium to fine*	Moderate	Poor	High	Plugs, sprigs, sod
Medium	Excellent	Poor	Low	Seed, plugs, sprigs, sod
Medium	Moderate	Poor	Low	Seed, plugs, sprigs, sod
Medium	Poor	Poor	High	Seed, sod
Medium	Poor	Poor	High	Seed
Coarse	Moderate	Good	Moderate	Plugs, sprigs, sod
Medium to coarse*	Moderate	Moderate	Moderate	Seed, sod
Medium to fine*	Excellent	Good	Moderate	Plugs, sod

*Depends on selection. Contact your local garden center for the best selections for your area.

COOL-SEASON GRASSES

Creeping red fescue. Although better in mild climates, such as the Northwest, creeping red fescue is the most shade tolerant of all grasses and is worth trying as a last resort under trees in the upper South, especially in cooler mountain areas. Flyer is a popular selection.

Kentucky bluegrass. Few grasses match Kentucky bluegrass for elegance and toughness, but the grass does best where average summer temperatures drop consistently below 70 degrees at night, typically in the higher elevations of the middle and upper South. The grass reseeds to form a thick turf, but it requires plenty of fertilizer for the lawn to maintain its plush look.

Perennial ryegrass. Perennial ryegrass is also used in the cooler upper South, but it takes much longer to form a thick lawn. Perennial and annual ryegrass are used to overseed warm-season grasses during their brown, dormant period. Perennial ryegrass is not regarded as a low-maintenance selection since it requires mowing through the winter.

Tall fescue. The tall fescues, a group of grasses made famous by outdated selection Kentucky 31, are versatile and durable. Improved selections are taking the lead for durability, fine texture, disease resistance, and drought tolerance for much of the South. They include Enviro, Falcon II, Finelawn, Houndog, Jaguar, and Rebel II.

Getting Started

Good soil preparation and proper planting will mean less work later.

One of the most reliable ways to reduce maintenance is to give plants the best possible soil in which to grow. Most plants can only be as healthy as the soil you plant them in, because the soil is the medium that holds water and nutrients for them to thrive. Unfortunately, the soil around a home may have been compacted by construction or be full of debris; often the topsoil has been removed, leaving only heavy clay or sand. Although you may view soil preparation as an unwelcome chore, it is always good insurance toward achieving a low-maintenance landscape. This preparation must be followed by proper planting and diligent watering, especially during the first two years.

Breaking Up the Soil

Good soil is loose enough to allow roots to expand easily. It is porous and well drained, yet able to retain moisture and nutrients. Organic matter, such as composted leaves, improves clay soil by breaking up the texture and opening it up so that roots can breathe. If you can roll moistened soil into a clay snake in your hand, it is too heavy and is likely to trap water around delicate feeder roots, drowning the plants or encouraging rot.

If your soil is poor and sandy, mix it with organic matter so that it will retain moisture and nutrients. Breaking up the ground and working in organic amendments throughout the bed will help your plants grow. Remember, the nursery-grown plants you purchase have been growing in an ideal soil; they will not want to grow in the poor soil found around many houses.

Never work the soil when it is wet, as it will dry in clods. However, you will find tilling easier if the soil is slightly moist, especially heavy clay soil. Water the day before tilling, or work the soil after a light rain.

Prepare the soil in stages to break up the work into several sessions.

Preparing Beds

Begin preparing your soil a couple of weeks before planting to help make the job more manageable. Soil preparation is the most labor-intensive part of planting and the most important. By breaking it up into smaller jobs, you can spread the task over several weekends.

Prepare the soil properly before planting to ensure that your landscape will not require too much attention.

A Place for Grass

You must properly loosen and till the soil to a depth of at least 6 inches to establish a low-maintenance lawn. Hard work at this time makes long-term care easier.

First, kill any existing vegetation in the proposed lawn bed by spraying with a nonselective herbicide, such as Roundup.

In a week to 10 days, you can break up the dead vegetation with a turning fork or tiller, rake it out, and add it to a compost pile. Till the area to break up compacted soil. Work in any needed lime (according to soil test results), starter fertilizer, and organic matter as you till.

Next, use a steel rake to remove debris or stones from the bed; then turn the rake over to smooth the bed so that it is even.

Finally, use a roller to settle the loosened soil before planting grass seed. Plant immediately after the soil is prepared; a heavy rain may undo your hard work if you delay.

A Bed for Plants

Mark the outline of a new bed by laying down a garden hose or drawing the proposed perimeter of the bed with spray paint. Check the outline of the bed with your lawn mower to make sure that it will not be difficult to mow around the bed.

You can transplant healthy grass to bare spots elsewhere in the yard or spray the entire area with a grass-and-weed killer or nonselective herbicide, such as Roundup. (This chemical will kill everything green, so follow label directions carefully.)

Use a turning fork or tiller to work the soil as deeply as possible, preferably 12 to 18 inches in heavy clay. Spread a layer of organic matter, such as compost, 3 to 4 inches deep over the area and work this until it is well blended with your native soil; use a turning fork or tiller until the mix does not clump in pieces larger than a quarter. Pulverized pine bark, which is often sold in bags labeled "soil conditioner," is an effective and inexpensive soil amendment. A carefully prepared bed

Regardless of whether you choose to sod or seed, you must have a deeply tilled, finely raked bed to grow a healthy lawn.

ALWAYS DO A SOIL TEST

A soil test is the initial step you must take toward making your landscape low maintenance. This test will measure the acidity (pH) of your soil and give you a reading of many nutrients that are present or lacking. A proper balance in the basic soil chemistry is essential for healthy plant growth; any elements that are low or missing will stunt plant growth. A thorough soil test will help you determine whether you should add fertilizers or adjust the soil pH.

Soil test kits are available through your county agricultural Extension Service office. The kit contains directions for testing, along with a form to record your findings. Most states charge a small fee, but it is well worth the cost to determine precisely what your soil needs to grow beautiful, healthy plants.

If you test in winter, the results will come back more quickly than in spring, when everyone else is also anxious to begin planting.

Sod provides an "instant lawn," but you will pay more for it than a lawn started from sprigs, plugs, or seed.

helps ensure that roots will spread through the soil. A good root system is essential to the health and vigor of a plant because the roots gather water and nutrients.

If you are planting individual shrubs for a privacy hedge along a property line, till a continuous bed at least 4 feet wide along the entire planting length. This will give you a single mowing edge to maintain; mowing between individual plants takes more time.

Planting a Lawn

If you are planting a new lawn or renovating areas of an existing one, you will need to choose between starting from seed, sod, or, in some cases, plugs or transplants. Cool-season grasses are often started from seed. Certain warm-season grasses, such as Zoysia, St. Augustine, and golf course-quality hybrid Bermuda, cannot be started from seed; they are established from sod, plugs, or transplants. However, a few warm-season grasses, such as Bahia, some Bermuda selections, and centipede, can be started from seed as well as from sod or plugs. Bermuda, St. Augustine, centipede, and buffalo grass can also be started from *sprigs,* or tiny pieces of stem with roots attached. These will spread as they become established. However, sprigs are probably the most difficult way in which to establish a lawn. With the exception of transplantlike *plugs,* or small pieces of sod, the two major choices for starting grass are seeding and sodding. Each has its advantages.

Seeding

Some advantages of starting a lawn from seed are the availability of seed and the ease of transporting it. Check with your local garden center for the seed or seed mixes and blends tailored to local conditions. After planting, you may store any leftover seeds in the freezer.

Sodding

Although sodding is more expensive than seeding, sod will create an instant lawn. Other advantages may make sodding a new lawn worth the additional money and time spent watering it.

- New sod is rarely patchy or uneven in color.
- Sod lawns do not erode or wash away in the event of a sudden downpour after installation.
- Sod is not as dependent as seed on seasonal timing.
- Sod is less susceptible to weed invasion.
- Poor areas in the sod can easily be replaced.

Planting Trees and Shrubs

If you are planting just a single tree or shrub, dig a hole at least twice as wide (preferably three to five times as wide) but no deeper than the root ball. Take the edge of a shovel and slice into the sides of the exposed soil in the hole. The looser the soil, the easier it will be for roots to penetrate it. Set trees and shrubs in the hole so that the top of the root ball is level or sits an inch or two above the sides of the hole.

Balled-and-burlapped trees and shrubs. If the plant is balled and burlapped, cut all cords around the trunk. Peel the burlap away from the trunk, and fold it down the sides of the ball after the tree is placed in the hole. Never leave the burlap exposed to the surface, as it will act as a wick to draw moisture away from the root ball. While cotton burlap will rot and the roots will easily grow through it, shrubs wrapped in a slick-feeling, synthetic burlap or in treated burlap need help. Make three or four vertical slices through the material before refilling the hole to allow the roots to penetrate the wrapping. Refill the hole with soil, mounding it over the sides of the exposed root ball, and water thoroughly.

Container-grown plants. The best way to remove a plant from a container is to turn the plant upside down and let it slip out. If roots have grown through the drainage holes, you will have to break them off or the plant will not slip out of the pot. When a plant is too large to hold upside down, lay it on its side on the ground and pull the container from the roots. Avoid pulling and yanking the trunk at the base of the plant as this can tear feeder roots. If the roots are matted and tangled, pull large roots away, making sure none are left to grow together in a circle. You can help matted root balls grow out of their mat by cutting crosswise through the bottom third of the root ball and then spreading the roots in butterfly fashion.

Planting in Soggy Soil

When planting in poorly drained areas, you may plant "on top" of the ground. After preparing the bed, dig a shallow planting hole so that the top half to three-fourths of the root ball sits above ground. Then cover by mounding soil up to the top of the root ball. Mulch with a 2- to 3-inch layer of pine bark, and keep watered. For best results, plant in groups, mounding the entire area.

Always set plants in their holes carefully so that they are never too deep.

Do not be tempted to plant young shrubs too close together. Neat mounding shrubs, such as dwarf yaupon, will knit together as they grow.

This technique works well for azaleas or any shrub that cannot tolerate wet roots. Wax myrtle and other shrubs that tolerate poor drainage do not require this treatment.

Spacing Shrubs

When spacing shrubs in a bed, you must consider the long-term life and health of the plants, not immediate visual effect. Here are some spacing tips based on a long-term outlook.

• If you are planting a large bed, place plants in a staggered or diamond pattern so that any three plants are the same distance from each other at the recommended spacing. They will fill the space more uniformly.

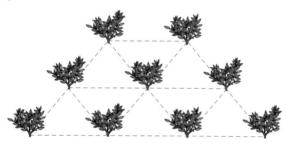

Planting in a diamond pattern gives a more uniform look.

• Do not plant any shrub that will grow taller than 30 inches next to the driveway at the street. You must be able to see over the plant for safety.

• You will be tempted to space plants too closely since small plants spaced far apart appear lost. Remember, they will close the gap as they grow. Stick with the spacing that will allow the plants to reach maximum size without crowding. Set plants at a distance nearly equal their ultimate size. Before placing plants in the ground, you may want to mark the location of each shrub with a stake or surveyor's flag. Write the name of the plant on a stake if you are working with a number of species.

• Very few shrubs (excluding some ground covers and vertical plants like nandina) will fail to grow at least 3 feet across. You can use this figure as the minimal distance at which to space new plants.

Selecting the Proper Tools

Taking care of a low-maintenance garden is much easier if you have the proper tools. Here is a list of recommended tools.

Bow rake. Use a bow rake (also called a gardener's rake) to level and smooth the surface soil in beds and to work fertilizer into the soil. Single-piece, forged heads are best.

Bucket. A 10-gallon plastic bucket with a handle, such as the ones used by contractors to hold paint, will come in handy for soaking plants before they go into the ground.

Fertilizer spreader. Spreaders ensure that you distribute lawn fertilizer evenly, which will prevent the grass from developing a streaked look. Use a broadcast spreader for a large lawn, and use a drop spreader when you apply weed-and-feed-type products so that the weed killer does not end up in your flower beds.

Garden hose. Buy a heavy-duty hose made of rubber or rubber and vinyl. Look for one that will remain supple, even in cold weather. A ⅝-inch hose is best for all but the smallest gardens. Good hoses are a wise investment for your garden.

Leaf rake. Pick a leaf rake that feels comfortable and lightweight and appears rustproof. Rakes with metal tines scratch through the surface of grass to remove small leaves and debris; they are also good for late-season cleanup and removing old mulch. Rakes with plastic tines, sometimes called lawn brooms, are lightweight and work with a sweeping motion. These are good for cleaning up dry, fallen leaves in fall.

Mattock. A mattock has a hoelike blade and an ax-shaped blade at right angles to the handle. It is used with a chopping motion. This tool is your best choice for breaking up heavy clay soil and removing roots.

Mower. While a townhouse garden may be maintained with a manual reel mower, a larger lot typically requires a power rotary mower. These can cost from $125 to $500. The best bets for low-maintenance gardening are mulching mowers that are adjustable so that you may cut the lawn as high as 3½ to 4 inches. Mulching mowers also eliminate the need for emptying a bag of clippings periodically while you mow. If you want a bagger, buy a rear bag model, which is easier to use.

Oscillating sprinkler. If you can own just one sprinkler, buy an adjustable oscillating type, which provides the widest coverage.

Pruner. Use handheld pruners for smaller shrubs and lopping shears for larger branches. Shears with a scissor-style cutting action are preferred over anvil-style shears.

Use a spreader to dispense lawn fertilizer evenly. This rotary spreader provides greater coverage faster but with less control than drop-type spreaders.

EQUIPMENT TO RENT

Most suburban gardeners will find that their need for a rotary tiller is too infrequent to justify buying one. If you would rather play golf than tend flowers or tomatoes, then owning heavy-duty gardening equipment is probably not cost effective. In addition, renting allows you the opportunity to try different types of equipment to see which ones best suit your needs. Other equipment that is often better to rent are a mulcher/chipper for small limbs, an aerator or thatcher for the lawn, and an edger if you do not edge the lawn more than once a year.

Shovel. The most useful shovel is a round-point shovel; this tool is handy for digging planting holes, shoveling mulch or gravel, and building raised beds. Another good choice is a narrow-blade (6 inches wide by 16 inches long) digging spade, which penetrates deeply and can be used to edge or chisel hard ground. Look for shovels with a long metal shank, a forged blade, and a grip handle.

Trowel. Choose a heavy-duty trowel that has a comfortable grip. There are various sizes for different tasks. Use a large-bladed trowel to set out 4-inch bedding plants and a smaller one for bedding plants from smaller pots.

A round-point shovel is a good investment for any gardener.

Watering can. If you have plants or containers that are not located near a spigot and garden hose, you will need a watering can that holds one or two gallons of water. Larger watering cans are more efficient, but these can get too heavy.

Wheelbarrow or garden cart. Either of these tools will save your back when you must move heavy items. The single wheel of a wheelbarrow makes it easier to move between plants but harder to balance with heavier loads. A garden cart can more easily balance a heavier load but will be slightly more difficult to work out of with hand tools, such as a shovel. If you plan to do heavy work, get a contractor's wheelbarrow.

Regardless of which one you prefer, look for sturdy construction, particularly in the handles of the wheelbarrow and the frame of the garden cart.

A rotary tiller will make it easier for you to till ground for planting lawns and large beds.

The Basics of Care

Low-maintenance landscapes are not no-maintenance landscapes. All plants, even the classic boxwood, need some care to look their best.

No matter how little maintenance is designed into your landscape plan, plants require water, mulch, and oftentimes fertilizer to stay alive. It is up to you to provide these. In addition, the health of your lawn is more affected by mowing than by anything else you do, so taking the time to mow your lawn properly will help keep it lush and free of weeds.

Watering

The most important thing you can do to ensure the success of a new planting is to keep it watered. At first, lay the hose at the base of the plant with a nozzle or water breaker on the end; a small sprinkler or a sprinkler system may not deliver enough water to a new plant where the water is needed. Later on, a sprinkler will be adequate for watering. One way to make watering easier is to weave a soaker hose among the plants in the bed. If the bed is longer than 20 feet, choose a hose less than ⅝ inch in diameter to guarantee better pressure to the far end of the hose and thus a better flow of water throughout the entire bed. Once the hose is in place, you can hide it under mulch.

It is better to water deeply just once a week than to give plants a shallow watering more often. To deliver a deep watering, you should apply about 1 inch of water each time. Measure this by setting a rain gauge or small can under the sprinkler (or soaker hose); when the water is 1 inch deep, you can turn off the spigot. Note how long it takes to deliver 1 inch of water so that you can set a timer on your spigot (or automatic irrigation system) to deliver this much every time.

How often you water will depend on your soil type and the temperature. Generally, once a week is enough to keep plants from suffering, but, in sandy soil that dries out faster, you may need to water two or even three times a week during extremely hot, dry weather.

Even a low-maintenance landscape requires some attention.

Often a plant will let you know that it needs water by failing to recover from midday wilt. If you want to accelerate the plant's growth in the heat of summer, you can water two or even three times a week if the soil drains well. Just be sure you apply 1 inch each time to ensure deep rooting.

Mulching

If you want a new plant to get off to a fast start, apply a 3-inch layer of mulch, such as shredded bark or pine needles, around its base. The mulch should extend at least a foot or two out from the base of the plant, preferably as far as the outermost reach of the branches. Mulch works to keep the soil moist and to keep weeds down. In summer, mulch helps keep the soil around the roots cooler; in winter, it helps prevent alternate freezing and thawing, which can affect plants set out in the fall. Most importantly, mulch conserves moisture in the soil, which is especially critical with new plants.

Mulch also reduces the number of weeds, but it will not stop all of them. If your schedule precludes occasional weeding, you might consider placing a porous landscape fabric around the new plants and then mulching over the fabric with bark. Such fabrics do not rot but are perforated to allow water and air to penetrate the soil. While black plastic is less expensive, you should avoid using it in the place of landscape fabric for several reasons. The mulch slides off it; the plastic blocks water and air; and, eventually, the black plastic will break up and become an unsightly nuisance.

Each mulch has characteristics that make it suitable for particular uses. These common mulches have their advantages and disadvantages.

WORKABLE MULCH IS A MUST

Inorganic mulches and coarse-textured mulches, such as large pine bark nuggets or pine needles, are difficult to work with in a bed that is reworked periodically. Therefore, it is best to use only finely ground bark in flower beds. It is easier to work with and may be poured into the bed. Also, fine bark mulches break down quickly, adding more organic matter to the soil.

Bark nuggets and pine straw are excellent choices for shrub beds where the soil will generally remain undisturbed.

Keep weeds down by using an organic mulch, such as pine straw. It also adds organic matter to the soil as it decomposes.

Bark nuggets. Large bark nuggets last a long time, but it is a difficult medium in which to work. Expect bark to float away in heavy rains and wash on slopes.

Finely ground bark. This finely textured mulch is by far the best choice for flat sites and flower beds. It is easy to work in and is readily poured or worked between bedding plants.

Shredded bark. A bit larger than finely ground bark, the elongated pieces of shredded bark last about a year. This mulch is fairly easy to work around plants and is very inexpensive.

Landscape fabric. Fabric mulches made from spun polyester come in several weights. They are permanent and provide a protective but porous layer that allows water and air to reach the plant roots. You can cover the fabric with a thin layer of bark or other organic mulch. Be aware that as the mulch on top breaks down, weed seeds may actually sprout on top of the fabric. Do not use landscape fabric in beds that are frequently reworked.

Pine straw. Fallen pine needles make an excellent mulch that lasts longer than fine bark. Pine straw is suitable for gentle slopes and for covering large shrub beds or natural areas under trees.

Plastic. Black plastic effectively blocks weeds but prevents air and water from reaching plant roots. Mildew grows beneath it, and mulches slide off it. Although plastic is very inexpensive, it will eventually create more work for you.

Stone or brick chip mulches. Stone mulches are popular in the Midwest and Plains states where the wind blows hard. They are permanent and provide a striking appearance but do nothing to improve the soil structure, unlike organic mulches. Stone can also look out of place in areas where the predominant mulches are bark and straw.

Place landscape fabric in beds where the soil will not be disturbed again after planting. Hide the fabric with mulch.

Fertilizing

Feeding with a controlled-release fertilizer at planting will give plants a head start on developing a healthy root system. You should aim your fertilization efforts at the roots since they are what will sustain the plant through varying environmental stresses.

How To Choose Fertilizer

When you buy a fertilizer, choose one that has at least 50 percent controlled-release nitrogen. Such brands may seem more expensive, but they are not. You are paying for the release of nitrogen over a lengthy period, which stimulates new growth steadily over time. Fertilizers that do not contain controlled-release nitrogen dispense all of their nitrogen quickly, rushing excessive amounts of the nutrient to the plant and into the soil, only to have it leach away. Controlled-release fertilizer is especially important for lawns, which have an extended demand for nitrogen through the growing season.

There are also many specialty fertilizer products that target specific plant groups, such as evergreens, azaleas, and flowering shrubs. Read the labels and compare the formulations to all-purpose, controlled-release tree-and-shrub foods. Sometimes you may target a group of shrubs with similar needs, such as azaleas, gardenias, and camellias, which need extra iron to maintain a deep green foliage. Or you may purchase a palm food, which contains both the magnesium and manganese used by palms; these elements are often missing from the sandy soil in the areas where palms usually grow. However, one universal tree-and-shrub food will serve most plants in your garden.

If you do not have any controlled-release tree-and-shrub food, you may consider an initial fertilization with a liquid root stimulant. Such a product will provide a boost after planting. You may also stimulate growth in shrubs, young trees, and ground covers by applying a liquid plant food every couple of weeks, especially in spring. Spraying the liquid food directly on the foliage will correct leaves that are yellowing from lack of food.

How To Apply Fertilizer

The most important thing you can do when applying fertilizer is to follow label directions. Products vary in the amount of nutrients and the rate of release, so follow directions to avoid overfeeding or burning.

Trees, shrubs, and flower beds. The easiest way to apply granular fertilizer when planting trees, shrubs, and bedding plants is to work the fertilizer into the soil so that it is evenly distributed around the roots. Or you can broadcast it over the bed after planting.

To fertilize existing shrubs, disperse the fertilizer evenly under the canopy of each plant. It is okay to sprinkle the fertilizer directly on mulch, as it will wash down through it.

You can apply liquid fertilizer in two ways. You may pour the liquid around the roots of the plants, where it will be quickly taken up by the feeder roots. Or you may spray the liquid directly on the foliage, where it will be absorbed immediately. Spraying the foliage provides a quick way to correct yellowing of plants in need of food; often you will see plants turn green overnight.

Lawns. Always use a fertilizer spreader to distribute the fertilizer evenly over the lawn to prevent uneven growth or greening of the lawn. A name-brand fertilizer will have recommended settings for spreaders. (See page 37 for more about spreaders.)

When To Apply Fertilizer

Although conditions will vary in different locations, it is usually recommended that you fertilize in spring, summer, fall, or sometimes all the seasons.

Trees, shrubs, and flowers. Spring is a good time to think about fertilizing because this is when plants experience a surge in growth. Generally, you should fertilize early enough in spring to take advantage of a full season of growth. While spring feeding is typical, many trees and shrubs also benefit from a fall feeding immediately after the first killing frost. Feeding at this time with a formula low in nitrogen, such as a winterizer product, will provide nutrients to the roots without encouraging new growth that could be severely damaged by frost. After the ground cools, a good controlled-release product that still contains nutrients will remain inactive until spring. Follow the rate recommended on the label.

Lawns. All warm-season grasses (except centipede and Bahia) should be fed through spring and summer. (Fertilize centipede and Bahia only once, in spring. You can increase their green color by feeding in late spring with a product that supplies minor elements.) If you cannot fertilize twice a year, a single spring feeding with a controlled-release fertilizer may be sufficient to maintain a healthy lawn. Fertilize after the grass turns green, and water thoroughly afterward.

Fall and early spring are the best feeding times for cool-season grasses. However, if you should fertilize only once, fall feeding is

THE FERTILIZER LABEL

Fertilizer packages list three numbers that correspond to the percentage of nitrogen (N), phosphorus (P), and potassium (K) in the fertilizer. A fertilizer package reading 16-4-8 contains 16 percent nitrogen, 4 percent phosphorus, and 8 percent potassium. Spreading 25 pounds of 16-4-8 lawn fertilizer on 1,000 square feet of lawn would feed it with 4 pounds of nitrogen, 1 pound of phosphorus, and 2 pounds of potassium. Since these are the nutrients that are most important to any plant, a fertilizer with all three is considered a complete fertilizer.

Fertilize shrubs, especially young ones, to encourage them to grow quickly.

TO RIDE
OR NOT TO RIDE

It takes about three hours to walk the 5 miles needed to mow an acre of lawn using a mower that has a 21-inch-wide cutting deck. A riding mower with a 42-inch-wide cutting deck will reduce this time by more than half; a larger mower holds more clippings, cuts a wider swath, and cuts at a faster rate. While the time savings are obvious, there are practical considerations to take into account when deciding whether or not to invest in a riding mower.

• Does your lawn slope? If so, a self-propelling push mower is safer.

• Are there a lot of trees to mow around? A push mower negotiates small spaces more easily.

• Do you have a place to store a riding mower? Also remember that riding mowers are not easy to service or transport if something goes wrong.

Riding mowers are a fine choice if your lawn is well designed, flat, easy to mow, and is one acre or larger.

most crucial to the health of a cool-season grass. Retail garden centers offer plenty of fertilizers formulated to suit local grasses and seasonal fertilization conditions.

Mowing

A lawn that is mowed properly is healthier and more lush, resists weeds, and tolerates drought better than a closely cropped lawn.

Mow at the Right Height

If you have to choose between letting the grass grow a bit high or cropping closely, leave the lawn alone. Scalping to "get ahead" in the lawn mowing will stress the grass and encourage weeds.

Every grass type has an optimal height. At this height, the roots grow deeper, making the grass blades more lush and resistant to weeds. The deep roots also help the grass survive summer drought. In fact, in summer you should let the grass grow one-third taller than the height recommended to help it compensate for stress.

MOWING HEIGHTS	
Bahia	2½ to 3 inches
Bluegrass	2 to 3 inches
Buffalo grass	3 to 5 inches
Centipede	1½ to 2 inches
Common Bermuda	1 to 1½ inches
Hybrid Bermuda	½ to 1 inch
Improved tall fescue	2 to 3 inches
St. Augustine	2½ to 3 inches
Zoysia	2 to 3 inches

Never cut more than one-third of the height of the grass at any one time. This will shock the grass and will cause it to brown.

Dealing with Clippings

Lawn clippings are an important source of nutrients. Recycling clippings by leaving them in place may reduce fertilizer needs by 25 percent. Also, leaving grass clippings on the lawn does not contribute to *thatch,* the accumulation of dead grass tissue between the lawn and the soil. To reduce maintenance, use a mulching lawn mower, which is designed to cut clippings into small pieces and scatter them over the lawn. These mowers work best if you cut the lawn frequently and mow when the grass is dry.

Problems and Solutions

No matter what the landscape style, certain problems are common to many locations and designs. Taking care of these with a low-maintenance solution will simplify your gardening. While the solutions to the following gardening dilemmas may not fully apply to your specific problem, they may get you started in the right direction. Then you can modify the ideas to suit the personality and style of your garden.

Overgrown Foundation Plantings

Overgrown plants at the foundation of a house may be the most common landscape problem of older homes. Typically, foundation shrubs extend well above window sills or are disproportionately large for the house. Often you must prune them regularly just to see out the windows. This often results in the shrubs being maintained as little more than large round bushes of little distinction. While there are no easy solutions, you can try to avoid the problem of overgrown plants altogether.

Solutions to landscape problems should make a property more livable with less effort.

A bed of shrubs and ground cover and a retaining wall define the entry of the house, reduce the size of the lawn, and level part of the slope.

Dig it up. The best long-term, low-maintenance solution to over-grown shrubs is to replace them with shrubs that have a suitable mature size. Severely pruning the shrub will just buy you time before you must remove it. There are many dwarf shrubs and ground covers that grow to only 4 feet or less. Two common ones for low-maintenance landscapes are dwarf yaupon and liriope.

Limb it up. In some circumstances, you may remove the lower branches of shrubs on the corners of a foundation and turn the shrubs into noteworthy tree-form landscape specimens. If the shrub is healthy, consider this option before removing the shrub outright.

Slopes

Slopes are subject to erosion and, if planted with grass, are difficult to mow and maintain. However, there are low-maintenance solutions to the problems of a slope.

Large, spreading shrubs. Large, spreading shrubs are a good cover for extensive slopes; their roots anchor the soil, and their foliage helps to break pounding rain. Shrubs such as forsythia and winter honeysuckle make an effective planting. Look for species that grow rapidly and develop vigorous root systems. Space them to cover the entire slope; do not prune, and let them grow together. You may need to control grass and weeds with weed killer and mulch between the plants until they cover the slope.

Ground covers. While ground covers blanket a slope, they are time consuming and expensive to establish. Aggressive ground covers that root where their stems touch the soil will provide the fastest cover. You will spend less time maintaining ground covers if you plant them where the slope is large and open enough to allow them to spread without encroaching on nearby objects or plants. Ajuga, Japanese star jasmine, common periwinkle, Confederate jasmine, English ivy, Japanese pachysandra, liriope, memorial rose, and mondo grass will all blanket a slope with a dense cover. To establish plantings on a slope, kill the existing grass by spraying with Roundup. After planting, mulch heavily with pine needles to suppress weeds.

Rocks as a ground cover. Short, very steep slopes can be effectively covered with rock work. One drawback to this durable solution is that

Limbed up into evergreen "trees," these dwarf Burford hollies that formerly blocked the walk and porch now frame the front door without obscuring the entrance.

the construction can look artificial and commercial if the work is poorly done. Also, the cost of installation can be high, and the spaces between rocks can harbor unwanted animals and insects. On the other hand, rock provides a natural look, and if you use local stone and set it to resemble native rock formations, the resulting rock-covered slope can cut down on maintenance and be an attractive feature.

Retaining wall. A retaining wall permits some leveling of the slope above and below the wall, creating a surface that is easier to maintain. It is an expensive solution and, unless the wall is less than 30 inches tall, usually not a do-it-yourself project. Consider building a retaining wall if the slope is otherwise unusable. The construction can result in an accessible, handsome landscape space.

Terracing. Long, steep slopes may require terracing, which is the construction of several leveled surfaces using multiple retaining walls. While labor intensive, terracing creates more landscaping opportunities than does a single, taller wall. This is because the terraces, however large, can be devoted to low-maintenance plantings. Terracing usually requires professional design and construction assistance. The technique is worth exploring if changing the natural grade in this manner reclaims otherwise unusable portions of the site.

Wet Sites

Low places where water stands after storms and persistently soggy locations are two tough problems that may make parts of a site marginally unusable. Unfortunately, water problems often require special equipment and professional expertise to solve. Here are a few ways to deal with too much water in your garden.

Explore drainage options. If undrained storm water is an occasional problem, a field drain or drainage pipe may correct the problem. If it is a chronic problem, this typically means the spot is simply too low to drain. The area will probably need regrading so that the water will naturally flow away from it. It may, in fact, be necessary to fill the low spot to eliminate pooling.

Naturally soggy soil may indicate a spring or other subsurface drainage (including a broken pipe) that is close to the surface. To eliminate this condition, consider installing a drainage pipe from the soggy location to a suitable outfall.

This stacked-stone retaining wall increases the usable area of the garden. The capstone also serves as a mowing strip. Perennial plantings, such as these coneflowers, soften the look and reduce weeding.

To tame a steep slope, construct miniterraces that may be used for low-maintenance plantings.

Choose plants such as Louisiana iris for areas with poor drainage.

Take advantage of the moss already growing in deep shade and damp, acidic soil to create a beautiful moss "lawn."

Build a wetland garden. Sometimes soggy soil presents the opportunity to plant a miniature wetland garden or a small pond. Consider excavating the problem area to better define its shape and merge it into the style of the rest of the garden. Seek out water-loving plants to fill the new planting niche that you create, and let the space become a focal point of a naturalistic garden scheme. Your wetland garden will be a low-maintenance feature since the plants will feel right at home in this damp habitat.

Use plants that can survive in both wet and dry conditions. Many times a landscape will have an area that remains wet during the rainy season yet is not soggy during drier periods of the year. In this case, you can create a bed or border of plants that can tolerate soggy soils for a short period of time but will not wither when the water recedes. These plants include bald cypress, canna, Louisiana iris, red maple, river birch, Southern shield fern, wax myrtle, and shrubs such as clethra and Virginia sweetspire.

Grow a moss "lawn." Damp, shady areas are often covered in moss. The moss can make a beautiful ground cover, and you can leave the area alone, only weeding and raking fallen leaves as needed.

Water and Wind Erosion

Both wind and water can carry away soil. You can eliminate the chore of replacing washed or blowing soil by stabilizing the soil with plantings and breaking the force of the wind or water.

Water Erosion

Water that is out of control can be a frustrating and even damaging landscape problem. If you are building a new house and are concerned about water-related problems, hire a landscape architect, engineer, or experienced contractor before you begin construction. It is easier and cheaper to prevent water problems at this stage.

Eroding water can be classified as either on site or off site. On-site water falls directly on your property; off-site water falls elsewhere and drains across your property. Erosion usually occurs when the soil is not covered and the storm water, flowing in a narrow stream instead of a broad sheet, cuts into the exposed soil.

Most on-site problems come from water running off hard surfaces, like a roof or driveway. Roof runoff pouring from downspouts with great force can erode garden beds, wash away mulch, and rut newly planted lawns. Either use black plastic drainpipe, which is easily buried in a gravel-filled trench, to carry the water beyond the locations it is eroding, or place rocks or coarse gravel at the downspout to break up the stream from the gutter.

Off-site water must be intercepted and either diverted or dispersed as it reaches your property. Depending on the volume of water and where it originates, off-site water can be a nasty problem.

Storm water runoff surging across a slope will erode the slope or wash away any mulch between plants. Usually only a thick ground cover planting can withstand the eroding waters. Until the planting is established, intercept and disperse or divert the water before it runs across the slope. You may find it necessary to construct a drainage swale at the top of the hill or install timbers or rocks in the soil to break up the flow of water.

Natural drainage paths that function during severe storms but are otherwise dry can be made into dry streambeds. These landscape constructions feature rock work that will not wash away and that can be an attractive addition to your landscape.

Wind Erosion

Sites where the soil is very sandy, loose, or thin are sometimes subject to wind erosion. Although more typical at beach locations or on the plains, wind erosion can occur anywhere soil is uncovered and winds blow steadily. A large planting of dense shrubs and evergreen trees that branch to the ground will serve as a windbreak, deflecting or partially blocking the prevailing winds.

Select locally adapted plants that are drought tolerant, since the wind also desiccates plants. Such a planting should either redirect the flow of prevailing winds up and over the exposed soil or deflect it over more stable ground.

At the beach, screen plantings can create a less hostile gardening environment by thwarting the killing effects of salt spray. Use salt spray-resistant trees and shrubs to create a protected environment for plants that are not as tolerant of salt spray.

Plants with tenacious root systems are also very effective for anchoring loose soil. Among the best at the beach are shore juniper and memorial rose, but there are many others. (See "Best Plants for the Beach" on page 61.)

Consider constructing a dry streambed to reduce the erosion caused by heavy rainfall. It echoes a real stream with great effect.

EDGES THAT CREATE WORK

Clear definition between different materials in the landscape always gives a landscape a crisp look. Sometimes the neat appearance requires unexpected additional maintenance. Be mindful of extra time involved in maintaining the following edges.

• **Brick on end and decorative concrete edge.** These need a mowing strip to save on maintenance time.

• **Mechanical edging.** A string trimmer or metal edger can be used to slice and delineate a clean line along turf edges.

• **Metal edge.** This heavy-duty, long-lasting edge easily contains mulch but is inconvenient next to lawns and requires additional weeding.

• **Plastic edge.** Black plastic edging lasts long and is unobtrusive but does not work well as a mowing strip; a mower will cut it.

• **Wood strip edge.** Often laid on top of the ground, this edge works well in woodland settings to contain flower beds or gravel or mulch in walkways; but the wood may shift, warp, split, and decay. (Sturdy, treated lumber, however, such as 4- x 4-inch posts, installed flush with the grade as a mowing strip, makes a very effective edge.)

Edging

In the ideal lawn, the grass is cut entirely by the mower because the mower's blade is able to reach all of it. Any need for regular cutting with a string trimmer usually indicates the need for a mowing strip around the lawn's perimeter. Consider installing an edge at ground level that allows the mower's wheels to roll over it so that the blade overlaps all the grass.

Brick or stone makes a dressy edge that works well with curvilinear lawn shapes. The edge should be level with the lawn for easier mowing. Mortar the bricks or stone to eliminate soil where weeds can sprout. Bricks that stand erect either on end or on their side form a fine edge, creating a distinct separation between a lawn and flower bed. Lay extra bricks in front of them for a mowing strip.

When set on edge, brick retains soil and mulch in beds adjoining the lawn and diverts storm water.

Treated lumber can serve as a low wall for beds, making a series of terraces for planting. However, when placed next to the lawn, the lumber creates an edge that must be maintained with a string trimmer.

Trees in the Landscape

Although trees can add a great deal of interest to the landscape, they can create maintenance headaches. Living with these stately specimens requires a certain amount of acceptance, but with a little planning, dealing with them will be easier.

Trees in the lawn. It is not unusual for a landscape with many trees to have some portions of the lawn grow weak and thin. Trees, especially large shade trees, not only compete for the same soil nutrients and water required by the grass, but they can shade the grass, making it more difficult to maintain an attractive lawn. (It is practically impossible to keep grass alive beneath American beech, American holly, Southern magnolia, and low-limbed white pine.)

A lawn with a lot of individual trees is also difficult to mow. Group some of the trees within a mulched bed with an easily mowed edge, or surround each tree with a bed that is tapered at two ends so that you may walk around it easily while mowing.

Aboveground tree roots. Aboveground tree roots make mowing aggravating. Tree roots remain high usually when the underlying soil has a high water table or is very heavy clay, and the roots need to take in oxygen. Some species, such as maples, are especially prone to this problem. If the tree is worth keeping, include the troublesome roots in a mulched bed. Or you may prefer to bring in a light, thin (no more than 2 inches) covering of topsoil and plant a ground cover, such as English ivy or common periwinkle, underneath the tree.

PROTECTING TREES FROM MOWER DAMAGE

Nicking the bark of a tree with power equipment opens the tree to disease or insect infestation. If the damage is frequent, you can eventually girdle the tree and kill it. Newly planted trees in open lawns are the most susceptible; protect them from damage by lawn mowers or string trimmers by wrapping the lower part of the trunk with a commercial tree wrap. Or split a section of plastic drainpipe, open it up, and let it close back around the trunk.

Also consider shaping a bed of mulch at least 4 feet wide around the base of the tree. Taper the shape of the bed so that it is easy to mow around. This eliminates the need to mow close to the tree, risking accidental damage.

Mowing is easier when the base of each tree is part of a large bed that is either mulched or planted with ground covers. Just shape the bed so that it is easy to maneuver the lawn mower around it.

Messy trees. Consider creating a bed of mulch or shrubs beneath heavily fruiting trees, such as hickories, oaks, and sweetgums, so that their fruit falls benignly. You may have to enter the bed in spring to pull up a few seedlings. It also helps to install wire gutter screens if you have such trees shading the house. Male pollen tassels, acorns, nuts, and the narrow leaves of willow oak fill gutters quickly.

Avoid planting fruiting trees, such as crabapples, around patios or pools. It is best not to have any trees near swimming pools. Pine needles can clog pool filters, and fallen blossoms of crepe myrtle can be messy as well.

River birch drops limbs, as does weeping willow. Do not plant these trees around a deck or patio if you find twig collecting tedious.

Goldenrain tree is notorious for its crop of seedlings, so plant it in a place where its seeds will be mowed along with the lawn or where beds are worked regularly. Other trees that produce nuisance seedlings include elm, cherry laurel, and willow oak.

Bare Soil in High Traffic Areas

The repeated impact of walking will wear a trail across a lawn by killing grass and compacting the soil. Eventually the soil will be completely exposed and more vulnerable to eroding, and the worn, unsightly trail may become a rutted path.

Swing sets. Few plants grow well under playing children, so do not try landscaping such areas. There will be time enough to coax lawn back after they outgrow the backyard. Before erecting a swing set or play structure, excavate a bed and fill it with either sand or bark mulch. These softer surfaces are not as hard as the earth or a lawn and will provide a better cushion for play. Be sure to make the bed big enough so children will not fall on edging.

Pet pens. Dogs are just as hard on the earth as children, and there is the additional issue of waste and mud. A surface of finely ground bark mulch can be cleaned easily and will not hurt the pet's feet. Keep the mulch as fresh as possible to reduce odor.

Shortcuts. Fighting a footpath can be a losing battle. If the shortcut is useful, consider making it permanent by installing a durable walking surface. If the route is a genuine annoyance, stop the traffic by erecting a fence or planting shrubs across the route.

Use large stepping-stones and plant ground cover, such as mondo grass, in the spaces between the stones for an interesting path.

Unwanted Views

In every garden it seems there is always a view that you want to hide. It may be a neighbor's work area or the empty space under a deck. Here are two simple ways to hide unwanted views.

Plant a screen. The low-maintenance solution to a distracting, ugly view is to screen it with shrubs that need little care. Treat this screen as an important part of the landscape. Instead of a row of shrubs along the property line, use several species of plants. Mix flowering deciduous plants in front of the evergreens to give the border seasonal flair.

Prepare a wide planting bed, giving the plants room to grow, and apply a good edging. This eliminates the need to mow between separate plants.

Add a lattice panel. Architectural elements, such as preformed lattice panels or other similar carpentry detail, not only provide screens beneath decks but also can create a storage area. As with any fence, be sure that the lattice panel meets the ground with an easily maintainable edge.

Lattice can serve as a structure for twining vines to climb upon. Do not paint lattice if you plan to use it for vines, since you will not be able to repaint it without removing the plants. Be sure to buy a pressure-treated panel.

WHERE POSTS MEET THE GROUND

Posts, whether for a mailbox, a bird feeder, or a decorative fence, can become unsightly with weeds or grass growing at the base. You can eliminate this problem by laying a 3-inch-wide border of brick, stone, or mulch around the post to serve as a mowing strip.

For long fences, consider a continuous bed of mulch underneath the fence, or install landscape fabric between fence posts to keep weeds down and reduce maintenance.

Create a privacy screen between adjoining homes with a row of tall, narrow evergreens such as these junipers.

Special Gardens

The specific needs of an unusual site can be minimized with careful planning and design.

Design small gardens so that they are easy to keep neat because the eye is drawn to anything out of order.

Some gardens are so narrowly defined by either circumstances of the site or horticultural requirements that they merit individual attention. While the broad principles of low-maintenance gardening certainly apply, these special places also benefit from gardening solutions that are specifically geared to their particular needs.

Small Space Gardens

The term "small space garden" refers to an area that is not only compact in size but usually unified aesthetically and horticulturally. The space may be defined by architectural elements, such as walls or fences along property lines, or it may be part of a larger landscape.

Small space gardens are often associated with the townhouses or row houses of older cities, such as Norfolk, Wilmington, Charleston, and Savannah. They can also be specialty gardens, such as kitchen gardens, that are part of a larger site. The increase in popularity of townhouses and condominiums is making small space gardens more common.

Courtyard Garden

A courtyard garden presents particular maintenance concerns because it is typically enclosed by the house and garden walls and serves both as a vista from the interior of the house and a place for outdoor activity. Common maintenance problems, such as weedy beds, may be easily overlooked in larger landscapes but seem magnified in the confines of a courtyard. However, the smaller size makes a courtyard more manageable. Here are some points to consider.

• Make sure the courtyard and any paved surfaces in the courtyard drain properly.

• Consider an irrigation system or a spigot in the courtyard to which you connect a soaker hose system to water plantings.

• Use ground covers instead of lawn grasses, if possible. Taller, grasslike ground covers mask weeds better than low, carpetlike ground covers.

• Invest in long-lasting, low-maintenance edging details for any lawn area in the courtyard.

• Select plants with appropriate mature sizes;

When planning a courtyard garden, carefully consider design and plant selection. Items in a courtyard are always on display.

overgrown plants are a common maintenance problem in courtyards. If the courtyard is less than 8 feet wide, use large shrubs that can be trained into tree form. These include star magnolia, sumac, vitex, and wax myrtle.

  • Install a gate that is wide enough to allow people, plants, and equipment to enter.

  • Avoid flowers that need constant deadheading.

Townhouse Garden

A townhouse garden may be enclosed much like a courtyard garden or it may simply be the area at the front or rear of the townhouse. The configuration of any individual garden depends on the architecture of the townhouse development.

  Because of its small size, a townhouse garden will require less maintenance time, no matter how intensely it is planted. For example, a 20-foot-wide townhouse that is 15 feet from a sidewalk offers only 300 square feet of front garden, the size of an average parking space. Such limited areas provide many opportunities for you to be creative, while keeping your maintenance tasks simple. Here are tips that will keep you enjoying the garden from the terrace or through a window.

MANAGEABLE PLANTS FOR SMALL SPACES

It is easy to overplant a small space. The low-maintenance trees and shrubs on this starter list can form the backbone of a small garden and will remain a manageable size.

Trees
Crepe myrtle
Dogwood
Hawthorn
Japanese maple
Lily magnolia
Redbud
Star magnolia
Sweet bay magnolia

Shrubs
Aucuba
Azalea
Cleyera
Florida leucothoe
Indian hawthorn
Leatherleaf mahonia
Nandina
Pittosporum (dwarf selections)
Yaupon (dwarf selections)

Townhouse gardens tend to be small, intensely cultivated spaces. Make sure that flowers and other plants are in top condition because they are in full view of the house.

• Consider eliminating the lawn altogether. The lawn may be easy to care for, but storage space for equipment is usually at a premium.

• Use architecture, statuary, water features, furniture, or a handsome paving pattern as the focus of a garden. These will look good during every season.

• Make use of the walls. Mount tile ornaments or terra-cotta planters, or plant climbing vines to add a colorful vertical dimension to the garden.

• Put down fine-textured shredded mulch. It is easy to weed and replenish, and it looks more polished than coarse bark.

• Install a soaker hose beneath the mulch for watering plants.

• Space plants properly and keep them neat. In small space gardens, a neat look will carry the appearance until the plants fill in at their proper spacing.

• Keep flower beds small, or limit flowers to large, easily watered containers. Choose drought-tolerant flowers, such as lantana, with a long period of bloom.

RAISED BEDS

You can create your own small space garden by building raised beds, which offer several advantages. First, they make it possible to display plants at different levels, creating more interest in a small space. They also provide a chance to improve the soil because, in most instances, it is necessary to bring in a planting mix to fill the bed. In addition, elevating the roots of the plants will help offset drainage problems. Lastly, cultivating and weeding in elevated beds is easier because the bed provides an edge on which to sit.

Make raised beds from materials such as pressure-treated timbers, brick, fieldstone, or flagstone that are stable enough to retain the soil that fills them. Typically, pressure-treated 6- x 6-inch timbers can be secured with nails to a height of 21 inches without interior reinforcement. Stacked stone walls, on the other hand, might not be as stable at such a height since it is only the weight of the rock that retains the soil. These stones should be at least 8 inches in width and depth or mortared into place. Leave gaps in the stone or drill holes in the timber so that excess water can drain away.

Do not build raised beds wider than 4 feet unless you can walk around both sides. It is difficult to reach all the way across a bed that is wider than 4 feet.

Combine garden ornaments with rich foliage to highlight small areas.

Gardens within a Garden

A landscape is divided into many gardens that work together to unify the entire space. Below are two of the specific areas of a landscape that you can treat almost as separate gardens.

Passageway Garden

A passageway garden is a transition space between different parts of a site. This space is usually narrow, and its main purpose is as a walk-through. The often narrow side yard of a residential lot is an example of a typical passageway. Unfortunately, such areas tend to lack attention and design but can be improved if you keep the following in mind.

• If it is a high traffic area, establish a paved walking surface with a simple design.

• Be certain that no construction traps water against the house.

• Make provisions to deal with any downspout drainage so that it does not flood the area.

• Use spreading ground covers that will grow up to the walkway (or between stepping-stones) to inhibit weeds.

• Provide easy access to utility meters.

• If the garden is contained by a fence, make sure the ground beneath the fence is covered with mulch or treated in another way that lowers maintenance.

Entry Garden

An entry garden creates the all-important first impression of a home. These gardens must direct guests to the appropriate entry comfortably in any weather and must serve as a visual welcome mat. An entry garden presents a special challenge to gardeners because it must look good all year. Here are some ideas for designing a functional entry garden.

• Make architectural elements, such as the walkway, rock work, benches, walls, statuary, or the front door, the prime features of an entry garden. These items change very little throughout a year and will carry the garden in winter. Invest in long-lasting materials of the highest quality—remember, you only get one chance to make a first impression.

• Rely on evergreen ground covers and vines for a plush look. These plants are easy to maintain at the appropriate size.

The narrow passage along the side of a house is often a wasteland. Turn it into a quiet walkway bordered with easy-care plants, such as azalea, aucuba, scilla, ferns, and woodland phlox.

A herringbone brick path and a variety of plants increase the visual interest of this entry garden.

A Few Shrubs for Shade

Although shrubs renowned for flowering might not bloom as profusely if you plant them in deep shade, they will do well in partial shade. The shrubs listed below require little maintenance. You will perhaps need to control scales, which may attack camellias, and lacebugs, which may feed on azaleas. (See pages 124–125 for more about these pests.)

> Aucuba
> Azalea
> Camellia
> Fatsia
> Hydrangea
> Japanese andromeda
> Leatherleaf mahonia
> Leucothoe
> Nandina

• Use annual color in pots to direct attention. Even in cold climates you can use an evergreen shrub in a pot.

• Where possible, set out a combination of evergreen shrubs to give your garden contrast in color and texture. The shrubs will add year-round interest.

• Use fine-textured mulch for the neatest look.

Special Horticultural Situations

Sometimes a site is so dominated by certain local conditions that the entire landscape is a "special situation." Here are three common situations you may face.

Shade Gardens

Few plants grow at all in deep shade, as anyone who has walked beneath American beech trees or in a forest of white pine well knows. A shady garden therefore requires very little in the way of maintenance.

If you have deep shade, you also are faced with the challenge of growing plants that will provide seasonal interest while remaining full in form. Shade gardens force a change in plant selection or the opening of the tree canopy to permit more sunlight for plants that require more sun.

Deep shade calls for white flowers to bring light into the garden.

One advantage of shade, particularly the very dark shade cast by a building, is that it all but eliminates the possibility of a lawn. This presents the opportunity to plant a ground cover that will not need weekly lawn care. In some cases, the preferred ground cover may in fact be moss. If this is the case and low maintenance is your long-term goal, you cannot beat having your garden made in the shade.

Shady gardens can, however, be subject to mildew, which may develop on walking surfaces, making them slick. Scrubbing with a mild solution of water and chlorine bleach will kill the mildew, but be careful not to get the solution on nearby plantings as it can kill them.

Hot, Dry Gardens

Sites that are naturally hot and dry, such as garden locations in the Southwest, are nearly as demanding environments as the salt spray zone at the beach. The severity of the heat combines with a naturally low rainfall and typically alkaline soil to make gardening a difficult task in these sites.

You should plan your garden so that the plants have a better chance to survive in such a severe climate. Follow these suggestions to avoid getting into gardening situations that require attentive care or excessive worry.

• Test the soil to determine any nutrient needs.

• Prepare the soil deeply. Incorporate organic amendments that increase the soil's water retention ability. The goal is to encourage deep root penetration to cooler soil and levels where water is less likely to evaporate. Plan to dig a minimum of 12 to 16 inches deep.

• Plant trees that will provide shade. Such trees will produce diverse planting conditions in the future.

DROUGHT-RESISTANT PLANTS

Once established, the following plants will tolerate drought. However, all of these plants must be well watered for the first two years after planting to ensure that their roots are well established.

Trees
Crepe myrtle
Ginkgo
Goldenrain tree
Live oak
Redbud

Shrubs
Burford holly
Crimson Pygmy barberry
Elaeagnus
Glossy abelia
Leatherleaf mahonia
Ligustrum
Nandina
Oleander
Wax myrtle
Yaupon holly

When planning a garden at the coast, choose salt spray-resistant plants, such as this Cabbage palmetto (a native palm) and dwarf yaupon (used as a ground cover).

• Create low-maintenance features with rocks or other durable materials that can carry the visual effect of the garden during the most severe heat.

• Group plants with high water demands in one location to minimize watering.

• Water very early in the morning or late in the evening to reduce water loss from evaporation.

Establishing a low-maintenance garden in a hot, dry climate requires using plants that withstand the heat, drought, and alkaline soil.

Drought-tolerant plants. Most drought-tolerant plants are either needle-leaf plants or broad-leaf plants with typically waxy leaves that reflect light. Also, many of these plants have foliage that is light gray or silver. Other drought-tolerant plants have thicker leaves with a fleshy texture; cacti and the succulents are perhaps the most well-known examples of this group.

Grasses. Native and ornamental grasses are among the toughest and most drought-resistant plants. In the Sandhills of the Carolinas, the native wiregrass *(Aristida stricta)* is as resistant to drought as Indian grass *(Sorghastrum avenaceum)* or prairie dropseed *(Sporobolus heterolepis)*. Consider incorporating these natives as well as other low-maintenance grasses, such as pampas grass *(Cortaderia selloana)*, into your garden and permitting them to grow to their full height.

Seaside Gardens

At the beach, plants are taxed by sun, poor soil, and the killing effects of salt deposited by wind. The closer a lot is to the ocean, the more likely it is to be subject to salt spray, and the more difficult it will be for woody plants to survive, let alone thrive. These conditions are acute on the oceanfront and diminish gradually within a few blocks of the ocean.

But do not let these harsh conditions discourage you. You can establish a barrier planting that will take the brunt of abuse, shielding the more tender plants behind it. Once the salt-laden winds are blocked or deflected upward, the remaining limiting factors in coastal gardening are the porous and poor sandy soil (which is often alkaline) and the amount of heat and sunlight the planting area receives. Keep your coastal planting low maintenance by taking the following steps.

• When you plant, amend the soil with organic matter. This increases water retention, reducing the time you spend watering.

• Mulch heavily; this also minimizes the need to water.

• Consider an irrigation system. Water does not linger in the coastal soils very long, and plants getting adequate moisture will be more resistant to the harsh conditions.

• Eliminate grass. If you must have it, keep it to a minimum and make sure to plant it on level ground.

• Make certain the planting beds drain. Even with characteristically sandy soils, achieving proper drainage close to sea level can be difficult.

BEST PLANTS FOR THE BEACH

Salt spray and poor soil make the beach one of the harshest planting environments. This is particularly true on the barrier island beaches of the South. On these sandy spits, soil is thin and summer sand temperatures may exceed 140 degrees Fahrenheit. Here are some evergreen plants that are able to withstand these severe conditions.

Trees	Zones
Cabbage palmetto (*Sabal palmetto*)	Zones 8, 9, 10
Japanese black pine (*Pinus thunbergiana*)	Zones 6, 7, 8, 9
Jelly palm (*Butia capitata*)	Zones 8, 9, 10
Live oak (*Quercus virginiana*)	Zones 7, 8, 9
Red cedar (*Juniperus virginiana*)	Zones 5, 6, 7, 8, 9

Shrubs	
Bayberry (*Myrica pennsylvanica*)	Zones 5, 6, 7
Common oleander (*Nerium oleander*)	Zones 8, 9, 10
Dwarf pittosporum (*Pittosporum tobira* Wheeler's Dwarf)	Zones 8, 9, 10
Dwarf yaupon holly (*Ilex vomitoria* Nana)	Zones 7, 8, 9, 10
Fruitland elaeagnus (*Elaeagnus* x Fruitlandii)	Zones 6, 7, 8, 9
Indian hawthorn (*Raphiolepis indica*)	Zones 8, 9, 10
Wax myrtle (*Myrica cerifera*)	Zones 7, 8, 9, 10
Windmill palm (*Trachycarpus fortunei*)	Zones 8, 9, 10
Yaupon holly (*Ilex vomitoria*)	Zones 7, 8, 9

Ground Covers	
Lantana (*Lantana camara*)	Zones 8, 9, 10
Lavender cotton (*Santolina chamaecyparissus*)	Zones 6, 7, 8
Memorial rose (*Rosa wichuraiana*)	Zones 6, 7, 8, 9
Shore juniper (*Juniperus conferta*)	Zones 5, 6, 7, 8, 9, 10

Plant Hardiness Zone Map

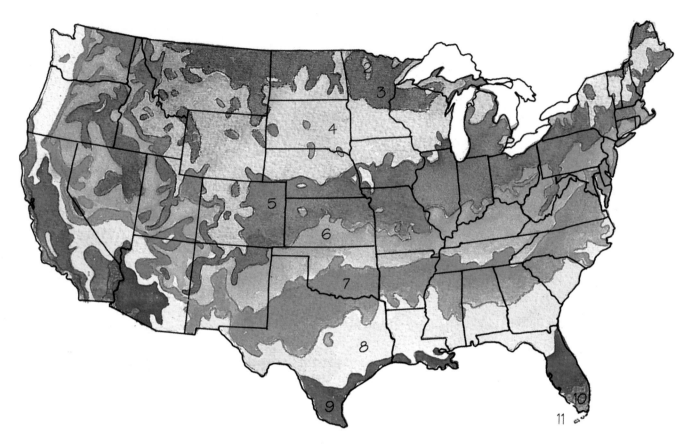

The United States Department of Agriculture has charted low temperatures throughout the country to determine the ranges of average low readings. The map above is based loosely on the USDA Plant Hardiness Zone Map, which was drawn from these findings. It does not take into account heat, soil, or moisture extremes and is intended as a guide, not a guarantee.

The southern regions of the United States that are mentioned in this book refer to the following:

Upper South: Zone 6

Middle South: upper region of Zone 7 (0 to 5 degrees minimum)

Lower South: lower region of Zone 7 and upper region of Zone 8 (5 to 15 degrees minimum)

Coastal South: lower region of Zone 8 and upper region of Zone 9 (15 to 25 degrees minimum)

Tropical South: lower region of Zone 9 and all of Zone 10 (25 to 40 degrees minimum)

Zone 2	-50 to -40°F
Zone 3	-40 to -30°F
Zone 4	-30 to -20°F
Zone 5	-20 to -10°F
Zone 6	-10 to 0°F
Zone 7	0 to 10°F
Zone 8	10 to 20°F
Zone 9	20 to 30°F
Zone 10	30 to 40°F
Zone 11	above 40°F

Plant Profiles

All successful low-maintenance landscapes have one thing in common, a well-thought-out plan for planting. To help you recognize which plants fit into your design, the garden editors of *Southern Living* magazine have carefully selected 60 plants to profile that could be part of any easy-care lawn or garden. For your convenience, you may find these plants in three different ways. The plants are grouped by type in the paginated list below. The profile section is arranged alphabetically by common name, and the Index lists both the botanical and common name for each plant.

Mahonia, holly fern, mondo grass, and impatiens combine to create a low-maintenance foundation planting.

Flowers

Black-eyed Susan, 69
Caladium, 70
Canna, 71
Coleus, 74
Coneflower, Orange, 75
Coneflower, Purple, 76
Coreopsis, 77
Cosmos, 78
Daffodil, 80
Daisy, Shasta, 81
Daylily, 82
Globe Amaranth, 87
Hosta, 95
Iris, 96
Madagascar Periwinkle, 101
Pansy, 111
Sedum, 117
Wax Begonia, 121
Zinnia, Narrowleaf, 123

Shrubs

Abelia, 64
Aucuba, 65
Azalea, Gumpo, 66
Chaste Tree, 72
Cleyera, 73
Euonymus, Winged, 83
Flowering Quince, 84
Forsythia, 85
Hawthorn, Indian, 89
Holly, Burford, 92
Holly, Dwarf Yaupon, 93
Holly, Yaupon, 94
Leucothoe, Florida, 98
Ligustrum, 99
Mahonia, Leatherleaf, 103
Nandina, 107
Oleander, 109
Pittosporum, 114
Rose-of-Sharon, 116
Spirea, Reeves, 118
Viburnum, Doublefile, 120
Wax Myrtle, 122

Trees

Bald Cypress, 67
Beech, 68
Crepe Myrtle, 79
Ginkgo, 86
Goldenrain Tree, 88
Holly, American, 90
Holly, Foster, 91
Magnolia, Sweet Bay, 102
Maple, Red, 104
Maple, Sugar, 105
Oak, Live, 108
Pine, Loblolly, 113
Redbud, 115

Vines and Ground Covers

Ivy, English, 97
Liriope, 100
Mondo Grass, 106
Pachysandra, Japanese, 110
Periwinkle, 112
Star Jasmine, Japanese, 119

Abelia

AT A GLANCE

❖

GLOSSY ABELIA
Abelia x *grandiflora*

Plant type: semievergreen shrub

Landscape use: foundation, mass, or screen planting

Features: glossy, dark green foliage; profuse summer flowers

Height: 3 to 6 feet

Width: 3 to 6 feet

Light: full sun

Water: medium

Pests: none specific

Range: Zones 5 to 9

Remarks: a tough, drought-tolerant shrub; attracts butterflies

A loosely trimmed abelia serves well as a hedge.

Abelia is a durable, semi-evergreen shrub that flowers best in the summer sun and requires little attention. This tough plant is called glossy abelia because of its shiny, dark green foliage. Its small but profuse white flowers appear in summer. Even after old blooms fade, bracts remain colorful until frost. If you shear abelia it will rebloom.

The plant has a loose, open growth habit with upright, arching branches. Abelias grow quickly to 3 to 6 feet tall and equally wide, depending on the selection.

Glossy abelia makes a good privacy screen, perhaps enclosing a yard or garden. It works just as well next to a wall or tall backdrop, such as ligustrum or Burford holly. Dwarf selections, such as Edward Goucher, grow only 3 to 4 feet tall and are popular for massing. Abelia also makes a good anchor in a large shrub border or foundation planting. Because of its small leaves, you can trim abelia as a hedge. However, this plant is best left alone, with occasional pruning to renew older growth.

In colder areas of its range, abelia will shed its leaves; many of the dwarf selections may be killed to the ground but will easily return in spring. This ability to withstand both cold and drought make it one of the more durable of the summer-flowering shrubs. However, for best results, plant the shrub in full sun or partial shade in moist, well-drained soil. It blooms most profusely when it receives at least six hours of sunlight daily.

AT A GLANCE

JAPANESE AUCUBA
Aucuba japonica

Plant type: evergreen shrub

Landscape use: foundation or screen planting

Features: glossy foliage, upright form

Height: 3 to 10 feet

Width: 2 to 3 feet

Light: shade to partial shade

Water: medium

Pests: sclerotinia leaf fungus

Range: Zones 7 to 10

Remarks: a dependable deep-shade plant with a tropical lushness; many selections have brightly variegated leaves; fungus problems not a risk everywhere; some selections bear large bright berries

The brilliant variegation of Japanese aucuba brightens shady beds.

Japanese aucuba resembles a houseplant because of its large, coarse-textured leaves. The species has dark green glossy leaves up to 8 inches in length on dark green stems. This shrub can reach 10 feet in height, but you may keep it at half that height by selectively pruning the tallest branches. Expect the plant to keep a narrow, upright form, although it may branch wider in response to pruning. Male and female flowers occur on different plants. If you plant male and female shrubs near each other, the female will produce bright red berries in the fall.

Japanese aucuba's irregular, multistemmed habit of growth makes it a good candidate for informal plantings, while its dressy foliage makes it suitable for formal settings as well. Try using it as an alternative to rhododendron in naturalistic plantings or as a foliage contrast with boxwood. Aucuba also works nicely in the narrow space between a house and a sidewalk or a driveway or as an accent in a shady courtyard.

Aucuba will remain full and handsome even in shade. The most popular selections are brightly variegated with spots or splotches of gold that brighten the shade. If you plant aucuba under the canopy of trees or on the north side of a structure, it will provide a lush, tropical look.

Plant the shrub in welldrained, sandy soil rich in organic matter. Soggy conditions will kill it. Be sure to protect it from direct sunshine as the sun will burn the leaves.

Azalea, Gumpo

Gumpo azaleas make an excellent ground cover.

AT A GLANCE
❖
GUMPO AZALEA
Azalea x *satsuki Gumpo*

Plant type: evergreen shrub

Landscape use: accent, ground cover, foundation or mass planting

Features: mounding habit of growth, profuse early-summer flowers

Height: 3 to 4 feet

Width: 4 to 5 feet

Light: partial shade

Water: medium

Pests: lacebugs, leaf miners

Range: Zones 7 to 9

Remarks: an excellent year-round evergreen; attractive foliage; a good choice for courtyards and planters; low growth habit; suitable for foundations

Gumpo azaleas are the most popular selections of the Satsuki hybrid evergreen azaleas. These low-growing plants not only produce an abundance of flowers in late spring, but they also provide handsome foliage throughout the year. Gumpos eventually become mounds of soft small leaves and reach 3 to 4 feet high and as much as 5 feet wide. Individual plants look like cushions. Although gumpos are slow to become established, they require less work than all other azaleas.

The leaves of this plant are less than 1 inch long and have a noticeably fuzzy look. Leaf color is a deep green with sporadic, scattered seasonal yellowing in fall. Generally, the foliage looks thick and lush throughout the year.

The flowers can measure up to 2 inches across. They open in late May to early June and may last two weeks. Gumpo azaleas tolerate direct sun better than most evergreen hybrid azaleas. They make a good ground cover in the sunnier reaches of a shaded bed.

Gumpo azaleas are most effective when you use them in drifts to create a sweep of blooms. Plant them in partial shade, preferably where they receive morning sun. They tolerate full sun, but it can distort their shape and size. In deep shade, evergreen azaleas may not bloom as much and they may get spindly.

When planting gumpos, be sure they are well watered before they go into the ground. They dry out easily, and once they do, parts of the plant may die back. Water gumpos regularly for the first two years, until the roots are well established.

AT A GLANCE

❖
BALD CYPRESS
Taxodium distichum

Plant type: deciduous tree

Landscape use: accent, street tree

Features: beautiful needle-shaped leaves, reddish bark, golden fall color

Height: 50 to 70 feet

Spread: 20 to 30 feet

Light: full sun

Water: high to low

Pests: none specific

Range: Zones 4 to 9

Remarks: unusually high tolerance of wet, dry, and poor soil conditions; grows quickly to a tall tree with a narrow crown

The fine texture and conical shape of bald cypress give the tree a stately look.

Bald cypress grows rapidly, maintaining an almost perfect cone shape in its early years. Although a 7-foot cypress can reach 20 feet in height in 10 to 15 years, it will not have a broad crown. Even mature trees, which may reach 50 to 70 feet, rarely have a crown broader than 30 feet.

Bald cypress has the needles of a conifer but, unlike most conifers, sheds them in the fall. The delicate, feather-like foliage gives the tree a soft outline. It casts a light shade, permitting lawn grasses to grow beneath the canopy. In fall, the pliable light green needles turn a golden brown before dropping to the ground.

Native to Southern swamps, bald cypress would seem an unlikely candidate for landscape use; however, its adaptability to both wet and dry soil makes it a wise choice. In the garden, bald cypress does not develop the roots above ground, or "knees," typical of trees in swamps. Because it tolerates poor soil, you can plant bald cypress as a street tree or around homes. It is also effective as a single planting at the end of a driveway or to line a driveway. Its narrow crown makes it suitable for foundation plantings, as long as it is planted at least 15 feet from the house.

Try planting bald cypress in groups of three in a triangle to enhance their conical form. You will find they are especially attractive when viewed from a distance. Properties with wet areas are also good locations for bald cypress.

Beech

The parchment-colored leaves of young American beech glisten in the winter woods.

The native American beech brings a year-round splendor to the garden. This long-lived tree grows slowly to 50 to 70 feet (sometimes 100 feet in the wild) with a crown spread between 40 and 60 feet that casts a very deep shade.

After the lime green foliage emerges from brown cigar-shaped buds in spring, the tree settles into its role as a deep green shade tree. In fall, the leaves turn an exquisite bronze gold, a color duplicated by no other tree. In late fall, the foliage changes to a warm parchment; in winter, the smooth, light gray bark of American beech becomes distinctive.

Branches bear silvery gray twigs that are finely textured and are angled in a zigzag pattern. The leaves are 2 to 5 inches in length; in summer, they are dark glossy green on the top and slightly lighter underneath.

Use this tree as an open-lawn specimen at the end of a garden vista, or set it in a border. To highlight the tree's silvery gray bark, place it against a wall or the side of a garage or against an evergreen backdrop, such as white pine or hemlock. Plant several beech together in a grove for a stunning look. Because of the tree's dense foliage and many shallow roots, you should plant only vigorous, shade-tolerant ground covers beneath it.

Give American beech rich soil, and water it regularly during periods of drought. Plant in full sun or partial shade. Eventually, beech will grow taller than many of the trees around it.

Black-eyed Susan

AT A GLANCE
❖
BLACK-EYED SUSAN
Rudbeckia hirta

Plant type: biennial

Landscape use: vibrant color for flower beds

Features: carefree growth, yellow blooms in summer

Height: 24 to 36 inches

Width: 12 to 16 inches

Light: full sun to light shade

Water: low

Pests: none specific

Range: Zones 4 to 10

Colors: bright yellow

Remarks: often reseeds; blooms from midsummer until frost;
looks good in both wildflower gardens and cultivated borders

You can always depend upon the bright faces of black-eyed Susan for color in the heat of summer.

Black-eyed Susan is a popular flower with gardeners because it is easy to grow and mixes well with other plants. The blooms are 2 to 3 inches across and appear from July until mid-September. The familiar yellow flowers have a black circle or "eye" in the center from which the plant gets its name.

Black-eyed Susan can be used in many ways in the landscape. You can plant it in flower beds, with shrubs or ground cover, or in a cutting garden. Consider planting a mass of them at the edge of a wood for a natural look. For the most visual impact, plant black-eyed Susan in groups rather than scattering them here and there.

Black-eyed Susans may come back from their roots year after year, but this is unlikely. They usually behave as biennials or annuals, growing a big rosette of leaves the first year and flowering in the second year. They drop seed at the end of the season. It is not uncommon to see black-eyed Susans colonizing fields and roadsides as a result of their prolific seeding.

You can sow seeds directly into the garden in early spring, or start transplants indoors about six weeks before the last frost. Black-eyed Susan grows best in moist, fertile soil, but it must be well drained. The roots will rot in soggy soil. However, the plants will tolerate poor, dry conditions.

Caladium

As these white caladiums attest, the variegated leaves of caladium can be as showy as flowers.

AT A GLANCE
❖
CALADIUM
Caladium x *hortulanum*

Plant type: annual
Landscape use: seasonal color
Features: large multicolored foliage from spring until frost
Height: 10 to 24 inches
Width: 10 to 24 inches
Light: full sun to shade
Water: high, especially in sun
Pests: none specific
Range: Zones 4 to 10
Colors: green with white, red, or pink patterns
Remarks: grows from a tuber, which is handled like a bulb; plant when soil temperature reaches 70 degrees

Caladiums are grown for their large leaves that color a shady summer garden with patterns of white, red, and green. They thrive in the heat, but their leaves always appear fresh, bringing a cool feeling to the garden in the hottest of weather.

There are two basic types of caladiums: fancy leafed, which are heart shaped, and lance leafed, which are arrow shaped. The unique foliage of each makes either plant a strong visual element in any garden. The colors and textures add contrast to a shade garden, brightening those spots not sunny enough for most flowering plants. Because some types may grow to a height of 24 inches, you can use caladiums to fill large areas. For the best effect, try masses of a single selection; or plant two complementary colors.

Plant caladium tubers or young plants in the spring when the soil temperature has warmed to 70 degrees, usually in May or June. Thin-leafed selections prefer shade, while those with thicker, more leathery leaves will also thrive in full sun, provided the soil is kept moist.

Caladiums need rich, moist, and well-drained soil. Water these plants frequently, especially those in full sun, and mulch the soil around them to retain moisture. However, do not let the soil become soggy or the tubers may rot. You may dig up the tubers before the first frost and store them for the next spring.

Canna

AT A GLANCE
❖
CANNA
Canna x *generalis*

Plant type: perennial

Landscape use: accent, seasonal color

Features: tropical foliage, bright flowers in summer

Height: 1½ to 8 feet

Spread: 2 feet

Light: full sun

Water: high

Pests: canna leaf rollers

Range: Zones 7 to 10

Colors: red, orange, salmon, pink, yellow

Remarks: dramatic appearance; good backdrop plant; tall selections among the boldest-looking perennials

Tropical Rose, an All-America Selections winner, is shorter and stouter than many older selections of cannas.

Cannas bring a striking look to the summer garden. Flowers open atop cornlike stalks in red, orange, salmon, pink, or yellow and continue to bloom from midsummer until the first frost.

Cannas range in height from 1½ to 8 feet, providing a strong, coarse texture in the landscape. Their large leaves may be emerald green, variegated, bronze, or purple. Give them room for massing at the end of a view across a lawn, a terrace, or other open area. In smaller spaces, plant cannas in groups of at least three to make them look fuller. You can use them in a sweeping curve or as a bold statement in a perennial border, a flower bed, or anywhere you want to draw the eye. Cannas may stand alone as accents in a small, enclosed area or a corner of a patio. Dwarf selections make good container plants because they remain small and will not fall over. They also are effective in flower borders.

Plant cannas in full sun in spring once the threat of frost has passed. Although they prefer rich, moist soil, cannas will grow in sandy or clay soil. They tolerate wet conditions and will do well at the water's edge. Cannas are generally cold hardy only through Zone 7, but you can grow them in pots and move them into a basement or a garage for winter.

71

Chaste Tree

Transform a chaste tree into a handsome accent by pruning its lower limbs.

Chaste tree, also known as vitex, is valued for its spikes of blue flowers. It is tough and resilient and easily rivals crepe myrtle's show, offering a refreshing cool blue color in the summer. In Zones 8 and 9, chaste tree will quickly grow to 15 or 20 feet high and nearly as broad. Farther north, intermittent extreme cold will kill back the top. In Zone 6, winters are cold enough to kill the shrub all the way to the ground, thus making it a perennial.

Regardless of height, chaste tree fills a void in the garden with its profuse and long-lasting flower spikes. The flowers occur on new growth each year and will bloom every summer, even if the top was killed to the ground the previous winter. The leaves are compound with five to seven leaflets that are green on the surface and nearly gray underneath. The foliage has a finely textured, loose look and is aromatic.

Chaste tree is best used as a specimen or accent plant. It can also soften the appearance of a wall or a garage. If you train it to tree form by removing its lower limbs, the tree will develop an irregular, slightly spreading crown. In this form, it is an unexpected choice for a terrace planting.

While most chaste trees have blue flowers, a few selections feature a different color. Alba and Silver Spire have white blossoms, and Rosea has pink blossoms.

Plant chaste tree in full sun in any type of well-drained soil. Water the shrub thoroughly to establish it the first year; then step back and enjoy the years of bloom.

Cleyera

AT A GLANCE

❖

JAPANESE CLEYERA
Ternstroemia gymnanthera

Plant type: evergreen shrub

Landscape use: accent, mass, foundation, or screen planting

Features: glossy foliage, tidy growth habit

Height: 8 to 10 feet

Width: 4 to 5 feet

Light: full sun to partial shade

Water: medium

Pests: none specific

Range: Zones 7 to 9

Remarks: deep black-green foliage reddens in winter; relaxed, refined appearance; good choice for a screen or courtyard accent; severe winter can cause foliage to drop

Japanese cleyera is prized for its glossy evergreen foliage and elegant form.

Japanese cleyera, also called cleyera, is an evergreen shrub that has a neat, upright rounded form with glossy foliage. It grows slowly to 8 to 10 feet tall and half as wide. This shrub has 2-inch leaves that are whorled around the tips of the branches. Although it is evergreen, cleyera goes through many color changes. Spring's foliage is a brilliant copper that darkens to bronze and then to deep black green in summer. In winter, the foliage takes on a rich burgundy color, which may turn a vivid wine red. However, during a severe winter, cleyera may drop its leaves.

The plant's creamy white flowers bloom in late spring, emitting a delicate sweet scent. Berries ripen to dark red in August and remain through winter.

Cleyera has a loose, casual outline that makes it useful for screening in formal and informal plantings. A fence or wall is an excellent backdrop for cleyera, which in turn serves as a partial screen for the structure. Cleyera is a good candidate to fill the corner of a small courtyard or to anchor the corner of a foundation planting. You can plant this shrub beneath a high-shade canopy for an informal screen, or use it as an accent in plantings of other shrubs with contrasting color.

Cleyera grows well in partial shade but needs protection from winter winds in the colder regions of Zone 7. It will tolerate a variety of soils but must have good drainage.

Coleus

Coleus keeps its bright foliage color from spring until frost.

Coleus presents only one garden problem—deciding which one to buy. Plants are available in reds, greens, copper, white, and combinations of each. One of the few annuals grown strictly for their foliage, coleus will contribute a variety of hues and textures to the garden. Many selections thrive in the shade, where vivid color is hard to come by, but many also do well in full sun.

Coleus will brighten a garden with foliage that lasts until the first frost browns the leaves. It is particularly handsome mixed with ferns and other finely textured plants in shady areas. Choose coleus for a splash of color in a flower bed on the north side of a house, where there is little direct sunlight. Or use it in a container, as it will fill out quickly in a pot. You will often find the duck foot varieties or other types of smaller coleus sold in baskets.

Plant coleus when the weather and the soil are reliably warm, usually at least two weeks after the last frost. Be sure to water, as large-leafed selections may droop in summer heat. You can keep tall selections fuller by pinching the tips of the stems every month or so as the plants grow or by trimming the stems back a few inches just above a leaf. New shoots will sprout from this point.

Coneflower, Orange

Orange coneflowers are held on tall stalks perfect for cutting.

The colorful, daisylike blossoms of this native coneflower thrive without pampering, putting on their best show in midsummer. An excellent plant for a border, orange coneflower is easy to grow and blooms prolifically. Its blossoms may also be cut for arrangements.

You can mass this rugged perennial along the edge of a wooded area, or use it in sunny parts of a naturalistic landscape. It is perfect against split-rail fences and mixes beautifully in a flower border.

This sturdy plant grows 2 to 3 feet tall and has coarse, dark green foliage. Orange coneflowers are actually more yellow than orange, with Goldsturm being the most popular selection. A profusely flowering plant, Goldsturm has golden yellow blossoms that are 3 to 4 inches in diameter. Its vivid color and open form make it a versatile addition to the garden. Since this coneflower spreads by rhizomes, a planting of Goldsturm will steadily increase in size, so be sure to allow plenty

of room for it to grow. Divide the clump every three years to encourage new growth and more profuse blooming.

Plant orange coneflower in full sun for best flowering. It adapts well to most soil types, as long as the soil drains well. However, this perennial will bloom best in rich, moist ground. Occasionally, in seasons of heavy rainfall, you will need to provide a support for the flower-laden stems, which may lean or flop in the rain.

Coneflower, Purple

The large blooms of purple coneflower have petals that often hang like a skirt, especially as the flower ages.

AT A GLANCE
❖
PURPLE CONEFLOWER
Echinacea purpurea

Plant type: perennial

Landscape use: accent, border, mass planting

Features: tall backdrop perennial

Height: 2 to 4 feet

Spread: 1½ to 2 feet

Light: full sun to partial shade

Water: medium

Pests: none specific

Range: Zones 3 to 10

Colors: lavender, pink, or white flowers with brown to orange centers

Remarks: rangy, stiff perennial with prominent cone in center; large flowers measure 4 or 5 inches wide

Purple coneflower is a sturdy, dependable perennial for a summer flower bed. This native plant bears a unique combination of lavender to deep pink petals and a stiff brown to orange central cone. You can also buy an unusual white selection, but it is not as prolific and vigorous as the more common pink or lavender selections.

The long-lasting flowers are quite large, as much as 4 to 5 inches in diameter, and they appear at the ends of long stalks, typically well above the foliage. This plant reaches up to 4 feet in height when in bloom. It is best suited for the center or back of a border or mixed with other tall wildflowers, such as Queen Anne's lace. Because it grows wild throughout the United States, this perennial blends easily into plantings at the edge of woods. However, purple coneflower also works well as the prominent feature in a summer perennial bed and mixes beautifully with many other plants. The stems will frequently grow up through adjacent plants.

Purple coneflowers grow best in full sun, although they will grow in partial shade. You can sow seed directly in well-drained soil immediately after the last frost. Pinching plants in late spring helps them branch and keeps them from growing tall and spindly. Fall is the best time to set out transplants.

Coreopsis

AT A GLANCE

❖

COREOPSIS
Coreopsis species

Plant type: perennial

Landscape use: seasonal color

Features: vigorous growth; profuse, continuous blooms

Height: 10 to 36 inches

Spread: 1 to 2 feet

Light: full sun

Water: low

Pests: none specific

Range: Zones 4 to 9

Colors: pale to golden yellow

Remarks: dependable, cheery, and enduring

The yellow flowers of coreopsis are a brilliant addition to any garden, blooming profusely in full sun.

Gardeners who design flower borders often rely on yellow coreopsis for a spark of color. This Southern native perennial is not only pretty and cheerful, but it also is drought tolerant, is not bothered by pests, and requires only an occasional feeding. To top it off, your strategic choice among the different species of coreopsis, also called tickseed, will yield a nonstop show of bright yellow blooms from April until September. For those who like the daisylike form and hardy nature of coreopsis but prefer softer colors, the threadleaf coreopsis *(Coreopsis verticillata)* offers smaller blooms, finer foliage, and pale yellow flowers.

Because the eye is drawn to yellow, choose yellow species and selections of coreopsis to brighten an area, establish a focal point, or draw attention from a distance. While the yellow-flowered species of coreopsis blend well with red, orange, and other warm colors, they also work well with blue, lavender, and purple, bringing these cool colors to life. Suitable blue companions include mealycup sage, Mexican bush sage, purple verbena, ageratum, and blue larkspur.

Most species of coreopsis are well suited to flower beds that receive little pampering. They grow in full sun and are flexible enough to tolerate both moist and dry conditions. Allow coreopsis a year to become established to produce the most prolific show of blooms.

Cosmos

Brilliant blooms on wiry stems are cosmos' trademark.

AT A GLANCE

❖

KLONDYKE COSMOS
Cosmos sulphureus

Plant type: annual

Landscape use: brilliant color for flower beds and open spaces where it can reseed

Features: heat tolerant; daisylike summer blooms

Height: 1 to 3 feet

Width: 2 to 3 feet

Light: full sun

Water: low

Pests: none specific

Range: Zones 3 to 10

Colors: yellow, gold, orange, red

Remarks: great cut flower; attracts butterflies and goldfinches

Klondyke cosmos provides a lift to the summer garden, with neon-bright flowers in yellow, gold, orange, and red. Easy to grow from seed in a sunny place, cosmos will quickly sprout to 1 to 3 feet or more. It will bloom through summer until the first frost if you keep it trimmed, as this prevents the flowers from forming seeds. However, because of its height, the one maintenance chore Klondyke cosmos may require is staking.

Use cosmos for mass plantings, or combine it with hollyhock, fall veronica, or purple coneflower. Use dwarf selections at the front of a border or bed or in a pot. However, this plant's foliage is sparse, so mix cosmos among more dense plants, such as creeping lantana, to conceal its leggy stems. Klondyke cosmos is often visited by bees and butterflies; its seed is a favorite of goldfinches.

Another selection, Common cosmos *(Cosmos bipinnatus),* is taller than Klondyke cosmos. It blooms in the summer, producing 4-inch-wide daisylike flowers in pink, white, or deep rose. Common cosmos has long, lanky stems and finely cut foliage that bring a soft texture to the garden. Plants may need staking in areas that experience strong thundershowers.

Cosmos is easy to sow directly in the garden in poor to average soil that is well drained. Scatter seeds on the ground without burying them. Be careful not to overfertilize or plant in rich soil, or you will end up with a lot of foliage but few flowers.

Crepe Myrtle

AT A GLANCE
❖
CREPE MYRTLE
Lagerstroemia indica and hybrids

Plant type: deciduous tree

Landscape use: accent

Features: beautiful summer blooms, upright form, showy bark

Height: 3 to 25 feet

Spread: 15 to 25 feet

Light: full sun

Water: medium

Pests: aphids, sooty mold, powdery mildew

Range: Zones 7 to 9

Remarks: long-lived durable tree; extraordinary variety in flower color and form; excellent for small spaces

Crepe myrtle is a perfect accent for most homes.

Crepe myrtle (or crape myrtle, as it is sometimes spelled) is perhaps the premier small tree for summer flowers, saluting the heat with a colorful show of blooms. In addition to its beautiful flowers, crepe myrtle is known for its handsome bark and surprising fall color.

Crepe myrtle is usually multitrunked and is available in many sizes. Medium-sized selections will grow rapidly to a mature height of 12 to 20 feet tall, with a canopy of 15 to 20 feet. The flower panicles carried at the end of new growth may be 6 to 12 inches long. They will often bloom again if you prune spent flowers as soon as they fade.

The many hybrids bear flowers in a variety of colors, including white, various shades of pink, red, lavender, and bicolored combinations. The best crepe myrtles are the hybrids resistant to powdery mildew, a leaf fungus. They include Catawba (dark purple), Cherokee (red), Conestoga (lavender), Potomac (pink), and Natchez (white).

Crepe myrtle is suited to many uses in the landscape. Choose large selections for a good shade canopy or live "fence" across a property line. Or plant single specimens as the featured tree in a garden. Trees planted in multiples are well suited to narrow side yards or beds of ground cover.

Dwarf crepe myrtles, which are not really trees, grow only 3 feet tall and work well as ground covers and in baskets and pots. Use semidwarf selections, which are 3 to 6 feet tall, as shrubs and in large pots.

Crepe myrtle is tolerant of poor soil as long as it drains well. Plant in full sun for the best flowering; even partial shade will diminish blooms.

Daffodil

You can depend upon daffodils to bloom every year.

Surely the species in the genus *Narcissus* are the best-known perennial bulbs. This group includes those flowers known as daffodils, jonquils, and narcissus. Most gardeners casually lump the many species and hybrids under the common name "daffodil," while enthusiasts can split them into 12 categories based on the arrangement and shape of the flower. What is indisputable is that their bright, cheery cups are among the best signs of coming spring.

The flower is available in an astonishing variety of colors and sizes. Plants range in size from 6-inch miniatures with 2-inch flowers to 2-foot-tall stems topped with massive 4-inch-wide flowers. But every type of flower has the same basic shape: a central cup, or corolla, surrounded by six petals known as the *perianth.*

These true bulbs are the premier perennial for naturalizing. The flowers are ideal for planting in drifts of 100 to 200 bulbs in a natural area or along the edge of a lawn. Groups of a dozen or more bulbs can provide a vivid burst of color in your garden.

Daffodils grow best in full sun to partial shade and require well-drained soil rich in organic matter. After the bloom is faded, allow the foliage to remain above ground to nourish the bulb so that it will flower the following year. You will need to dig and divide the bulbs every three to five years. Work Bulb Booster 9-9-6 fertilizer into the soil at planting and again after the bulbs bloom to increase flowering.

AT A GLANCE

SHASTA DAISY
Chrysanthemum x *superbum*

Plant type: perennial

Landscape use: accent, border, mass planting

Features: prolific blooms from spring to summer

Height: 8 to 30 inches

Spread: 8 to 24 inches

Light: full sun

Water: medium to low

Pests: none specific

Range: Zones 4 to 9

Colors: white with yellow centers, varieties in flower form and height

Remarks: a sentimental spring to early-summer favorite; bright, cheery daisy flowers; good for cutting

Shasta daisy's bright white petals and dashing yellow center make it one of the garden's most cheerful flowers for cutting.

Shasta daisies may be the most familiar of all flowers, flourishing cheerfully in gardens across the country. The white ray "petals" surrounding yellow centers open in late spring and early summer; flowers may be single or double, depending on the selection. The deep green foliage is evergreen in the lower and coastal South. Plants range in height from 8 to 30 inches.

This perennial has a simplicity that marries well with stronger, brighter flowers in beds and borders. Its flat, round blooms contrast nicely with the upright, vertical spikes of salvia or larkspur. The yellow centers mix well with other yellow flowers in the garden. Because it reseeds, this perennial is a good choice for naturalizing a wildflower garden, a meadow, or another low-maintenance location. Shasta daisy is the classic garden flower and always looks good against a wall or a fence.

Plant Shasta daisies in full sun or light shade. They require moderately fertile, well-drained soil and moisture for growth and longer-lasting flowers. To keep plants tidy, cut them back after they bloom. Divide clumps every three years when they become crowded. This will keep plants vigorous and blooming profusely.

Daylily

Daylilies are perfect for borders.

Daylilies have earned the nickname the lazy gardener's flower because once planted, they will flower and multiply with little care. When the showy blooms are gone, the fan-shaped foliage characteristic of many selections lends its green, grassy curving lines to the landscape.

Thanks to plant breeders, daylilies are no longer limited to the tawny daylily, the tall plant with orange blooms that thrives along roadsides. Hybrids for landscaping range in color from cream, yellow, orange, apricot, pink, lavender, and red to near-black; bicolored selections are available, too. Many are reblooming types that will flower for several months. With so many hybrids available, it is possible to have continuous blooms for 3 to 10 months, depending on the length of the frost-free season in your area. Although the bloom lasts only a day, each *scape,* or flowering stalk, has several flower buds that bloom in succession.

Daylilies are effective planted in drifts in a border of mixed flowers or shrubs. Daffodils and daylilies are ideal companions. The daffodils bloom first; then the daylily foliage emerges to hide the daffodil's yellowing leaves. Use daylilies for mass planting. The tougher selections will spread to naturalize an area and will help stabilize the soil on steep slopes.

Daylilies do well in full sun but tolerate partial shade. Give them rich, well-drained soil. Every two to three years, divide daylilies in the fall and create new beds.

Euonymus, Winged

A row of dwarf winged euonymus grows into a striking low-maintenance hedge that lights the fall landscape.

The brilliant red fall color of winged euonymus earns the plant its other common name—burning bush. A versatile shrub best known for its fall show, winged euonymus is unassuming in summer, when its vase-shaped form and finely textured foliage are easily overlooked. Long, corky growths project along its branches, giving the leafless shrub a sculptural appearance and also the common name winged euonymus.

When the foliage drops (usually in 3 to 4 weeks), clusters of tiny fruiting capsules split to reveal an orange fruit, adding late fall color to this large shrub.

As it matures, the plant assumes its identifiable vase shape, with branches arching to nearly touch the ground. Eventually, it grows to at least 15 feet tall and just as wide. Large shrubs may be trained into a tree form by removing the lower branches. The dwarf form, *Euonymus alata* Compacta, is about 10 feet tall and equally wide, with a more rounded and compact shape.

Winged euonymus is a splendid choice for an informal hedge or a mass planting or for a seasonal accent at the edge of a natural area. A backdrop of evergreens, such as cryptomeria, hemlock, or spruce, makes the color seem more intense, as does a neutral backdrop, such as a weathered wood or a gray wall.

Plant winged euonymus in well-drained soil. It does not like wet sites. You will need to water it, however, during periods of drought. Although the plant will grow in light shade, full sun will produce better fall color.

Flowering Quince

Flowering quince is one of the first shrubs to bloom in spring.

Although it blooms for a short time, flowering quince is one of the most memorable shrubs in the garden. Its flowers signal the coming of spring, blooming with the first warm spell in late winter. A rugged tangle of spines, twigs, and blossoms, quince's sculptural branches are prized for cutting.

The simple flowers of quince range from pure white to shades of orange and red. The blossoms are borne singly and in clusters along bare, spiny branches a few weeks before the foliage appears. The blooms resist frost, continuing for almost a month in sporadic displays. The shrub grows quickly into a large, upright, rounded plant, usually reaching 6 to 10 feet tall and equally wide.

In spring and summer, quince is covered in deep green foliage that often drops in late summer, revealing yellow ping-pong ball-sized fruit. The remaining leaves turn lemon yellow in the fall.

Use flowering quince in a shrub border with other plants or at the edge of woods. It is very effective in spring in front of dark evergreens. There are many selections of quince, some of which are hybrids of the dwarf lesser flowering quince *(Chaenomeles japonica)*. Cameo has double apricot-colored flowers, Nivalis is a white plant, and Texas Scarlet has vivid red flowers.

Give quince full sun for profuse flowers, but it will grow in partial shade. A rugged plant, quince will tolerate the heat on the south and west side of a building. It needs well-drained soil but does not mind either sand or clay, as long as it is not allowed to stand in water.

AT A GLANCE

❖

FORSYTHIA

Forsythia x *intermedia*

Plant type: deciduous shrub

Landscape use: accent, mass or screen planting

Features: yellow flowers in late winter and early spring; thick, dark green foliage

Height: 3 to 10 feet

Width: 5 to 12 feet

Light: full sun

Water: medium

Pests: none specific

Range: Zones 5 to 9

Remarks: superb, carefree plant, but needs room; excellent for steep slopes, for naturalizing, or along fences; makes an effective screen; many selections; best if unpruned

Forsythia sports a graceful arching form.

There are many hybrids of forsythia, but all share a gently arching form and spreading habit of growth. The shoots of an immature plant tend to grow straight up, producing a spiky effect. As the shrub ages, the branches lengthen and droop in graceful curves. At its full height and spread, forsythia may be between 3 and 10 feet tall and 5 and 12 feet wide, depending on the selection. The 3- to 5-inch-long green leaves turn yellow-green and sometimes maroon in fall. And just when you think gray winter skies will never end, this favorite shrub bursts into bloom.

Forsythia is dazzling in the early spring. Whether you plant several as an informal hedge or use a single plant to accent a border, this shrub is ideal for distant garden locations. It looks great beyond a window, where its blooming branches are silhouetted against darker backdrops, such as woods, walls, or fences. It also grows large enough and dense enough to serve as a privacy screen. Forsythia works well with evergreen shrubs, such as wax myrtle or ligustrum, or combined with loblolly pine or Leyland cypress to create a free-flowing border. Give it plenty of room to spread.

Forsythia requires full sun for best bloom. It grows in almost any type of soil and, once established, requires little attention.

Ginkgo

Ginkgo is a durable landscape tree with a distinct golden fall color.

Gardeners treasure ginkgo for its glorious fall color, unusual form, and uniquely shaped leaves. This rugged tree can tolerate urban conditions and consequently is widely used as a street tree.

Ginkgo grows slowly, branching erratically at first, but will become a full, large shade tree. A mature ginkgo grows anywhere from 50 to 80 feet tall and 30 to 40 feet wide.

The tree's leaves emerge bright green in early spring, opening into a characteristic 2- to 3½-inch-long fan shape that is divided into two lobes. The foliage remains a bright green until fall, when it turns a glorious golden yellow.

Ginkgo is an ideal tree for large properties or gardens where a corner may be reserved to allow ginkgo to develop fully. A group of these trees works well along driveways, where they serve as landscape features on the way to the house. Plant a single specimen in a prominent space in the open lawn or on the crown of a hill.

The only drawback to ginkgo is that the female tree produces fruit with a strong, unpleasant odor, almost like rotten eggs. Although the fruit may not appear for 20 years, you should plant only male trees. To avoid the female ginkgo, buy named selections, such as Princeton Sentry, which ensures that the tree is male. Do not buy unnamed selections.

Give ginkgo a spot in full sun and provide well-drained soil. It is tolerant of poor conditions as long as the soil drains well.

Globe Amaranth

Bright cloverlike flowers of globe amaranth bloom from summer until frost.

Globe amaranth is prized for its production of hundreds of colorful, cloverlike blooms that rarely fade, even under the brunt of summer heat. Undaunted by high temperatures, each flower retains its vivid color of purple, pink, white, orange, or red.

Use globe amaranth in flower beds, for edgings, or in containers. Dwarf types work well in pots and window boxes because they are compact and drought tolerant. Any selection will work nicely in front of taller annuals, such as common zinnias. Combine purple globe amaranth with black-eyed Susan or orange narrowleaf zinnia for vivid contrast, or plant lavender selections with silver dusty miller for a softer look. In addition to attracting the eye, the blooms of globe amaranth attract butterflies.

Globe amaranth also has added value as a dried flower. The papery blooms may retain their pigment for up to a year after cutting, making them quite popular for dried arrangements, wreaths, and other crafts. Up close, the flowers appear to be made of rice paper.

Plant globe amaranth in the spring from transplants or from seed sown directly in the garden. Make sure you plant it in well-drained soil in a sunny location. It tolerates poor, sandy soil or heavy clay as long as it drains well.

Goldenrain Tree

Goldenrain tree, also known as varnish tree, opens profuse panicles of bright yellow flowers in June.

In the garden trade this small tree is known as goldenrain tree, a reference to its midsummer profusion of flowers. However, some refer to this ornamental tree as varnish tree. It grows at a moderate to rapid rate to a height of 15 to 40 feet and a width of 15 to 30 feet. The tree's crown is rounded and symmetrical and is shaped like an umbrella.

Goldenrain tree features compound leaves that have a handsome, almost fernlike, look; these leaves are medium green in summer and change to a modest yellow in fall. In midsummer, the tree sports a showy covering of upright panicles of yellow flowers. The flowers quickly ripen into unusual clusters of papery pods, which are first green and then parchment colored and eventually dark brown. A related species *Koelreuteria bipinnata* blooms later and bears striking reddish bronze seed capsules.

Goldenrain tree is an excellent choice for planters or terraces. The tree's umbrella shape works well around patios. Its foliage creates a light shade that is ideal for growing perennials. Because it tolerates heat and drought, goldenrain tree makes a good specimen for streets or parking lots.

Plant goldenrain tree in well-drained soil and give it full sun. It thrives without much care after the roots are established.

Hawthorn, Indian

AT A GLANCE
❖
INDIAN HAWTHORN
Raphiolepis indica

Plant type: evergreen shrub

Landscape use: accent, ground cover, foundation or mass planting

Features: evergreen foliage, profuse fragrant flowers

Height: 4 to 10 feet

Width: 4 to 10 feet

Light: full sun

Water: medium to low

Pests: leaf spot

Range: Zones 8 to 10

Remarks: salt-spray resistant; mounding growth habit makes it excellent for ground covers or massing; flower colors vary from white to deep pink

Indian hawthorn is one of the better shrubs for coastal areas of the South, enduring even ocean spray.

You can count on Indian hawthorn to provide an attractive display of bright flowers and lush evergreen foliage in sunny gardens. Easy to grow, Indian hawthorn has a naturally neat appearance. It tolerates heat, humidity, and salt spray, making it a good choice for the lower South. The plant fills the same landscape niche in full sun and heat that azaleas fill in the shade.

The dwarf variety of Indian hawthorn will slowly mature into a low, compact mound, typically 4½ feet in height with a nearly equal spread. Its leaves are a dark, glossy green that reflect the sunlight. Flowering typically occurs in mid- to late April, and the blooms range in color from white to deep pink. The flowers are followed in late summer by dull blue berries.

Combine low-growing selections of Indian hawthorn with plants that have a similar growth habit to create an attractive border or foundation planting. In the lower South, Indian hawthorn works well near patios and swimming pools. Use it to edge a border of tall shrubs, such as wax myrtle, or drift several Indian hawthorns in an open lawn.

This shrub is an excellent container plant, since the roots do not suffer in constricted space. It is ideal for the coastal zones, for it loves the heat and will adapt to sandy soil and salt spray. Once established, Indian hawthorn is drought tolerant but will need a steady amount of water to get started.

Holly

American holly is a classic evergreen tree that will help anchor a landscape during the leafless winter months.

Best known for its spiny leaves and red berries, American holly is a classic evergreen tree. Like many hollies, the male and female flowers appear on separate plants with the female flower producing the berries. To guarantee berries, plant male hollies within 30 to 40 yards of the female plants.

American holly is native to the South. It grows slowly to at least 25 feet but can be as tall as 50 feet. It has a pyramidal form, which can be 18 to 40 feet wide at the base.

It has green, spiny leaves and light gray bark. In full sun, the tree is dense with its foliage noticeably layered. In partial shade or full shade, the tree has a much more open growth habit.

American holly and its hybrids make an excellent feature plant when used either singly or grouped in the landscape. It is particularly effective as a freestanding lawn specimen. Allow American holly's lower limbs to drape to the ground to achieve the tree's full, graceful form.

Because the native American holly is large, many of its smaller hybrids have become more popular. Foster holly, one of the most widely used holly hybrids, is more narrow than American holly and has a distinct pyramidal shape. It grows rapidly to between 25 and 40 feet high and 10 to 15 feet wide. The leaves, which are glossy deep green with a slightly blue cast, are more narrow and have fewer spines than American holly. While there are several Foster hybrids, Foster #2 and #3 are

AT A GLANCE

❖

FOSTER HOLLY
Ilex x *attenuata* Foster # 2

Plant type: evergreen tree

Landscape use: accent, screen planting

Features: narrow, dark green leaves; profuse berries; narrow form

Height: 25 to 40 feet

Spread: 10 to 15 feet

Light: full sun to partial shade

Water: medium

Pests: none specific

Range: Zones 6 to 9

Remarks: a fine-textured, fast-growing holly; stately, smaller size makes it suitable for smaller properties; serves as excellent screen in narrow spaces

Foster holly is one of several holly hybrids popular for their small size and prolific crop of red berries.

female plants that reliably produce large crops of berries. These hybrids are usually labeled simply as Foster holly. Foster #4 is a male plant which, if planted nearby, helps berry production.

Another hybrid, East Palatka, has rounded leaves and a loose, pyramidal shape. It grows to about 30 feet tall. Savannah holly has leaves with few spines and grows quickly to a height of about 30 feet.

The hybrid hollies, such as Foster, East Palatka, and Savannah, work better on small lots than American holly. Use these hollies for screening between adjoining properties or in a shrub border. As they mature, these smaller hollies can make good open-lawn specimens on a small lot. Their narrow form may lead you to think that they will work well in foundation plantings. However, because of their rapid growth habit, a tree placed too close to the house will lean away from the building. To avoid this problem, be sure to plant these narrow hollies at least 8 feet away from the house.

Hollies need full sun to fruit heavily, but they will grow in partial shade. They do not like soggy soil, so be sure to plant them in a location with good drainage. Hollies prefer rich soil, but they will also grow in poor, sandy soil. If you plant American holly in poor soil, be sure to fertilize it at least once a year to keep the leaves a rich shade of green.

Holly, Burford

Dwarf Burford holly is a good choice for creating a dense green wall.

Burford holly is one of the most reliable and widely planted of the Chinese hollies, a testimony to its attractiveness and vigor. This medium-to-large shrub combines handsome dark green foliage and large, bright orange-red berries with rapid, disease-free growth. It thrives in the hottest locations.

Burford holly develops quickly into a full, coarse-textured plant, easily reaching 15 to 20 feet in less than 20 years. Its glossy, dark green leaves are 1½ to 3 inches long and have a single spine at the end. The shrub produces abundant clusters of ¼-inch berries that provide a colorful show in the fall. Dwarf Burford holly, an excellent smaller-leafed selection, grows to a height of 8 to 12 feet.

If there is a secret to this shrub, it is to give it room to grow. Burford holly is too large for foundation plantings unless you prune it into a tree form. The plant is best used where it can grow to become a living wall or screen. Place it along a property line, and use it as a large natural-form hedge. Avoid shearing it since the wide glossy leaves turn brown at the edge when cut.

Burford holly will grow in clay or sand, but it must have good drainage. To grow dense and full, it needs plenty of sun. It can tolerate light shade, but it may not fill out as much.

AT A GLANCE

❖

DWARF YAUPON HOLLY
Ilex vomitoria Nana

Plant type: evergreen shrub

Landscape use: foundation or mass planting, ground cover

Features: low, cushionlike growth habit; small shiny leaves

Height: 3 to 5 feet

Width: 4 to 10 feet

Light: full sun to partial shade

Water: low

Pests: none specific

Range: Zones 7 to 10

Remarks: a drought- and heat-tolerant shrub that remains neat; excellent for the beach; a good choice for a low-growing foundation planting

Rounded, dense, and low growing, these three dwarf yaupons provide an evergreen entry to a rose garden.

Dwarf yaupon is a durable evergreen shrub that grows into a deep green cushion that is uniformly wider than it is tall. Mature plants may attain heights of 3 to 5 feet and can be as wide as 10 feet, although 4 to 5 feet is more common. These living mounds are densely covered with small, dark green leaves, usually less than 1 inch in length, that grow on a tightly knitted mesh of gray twigs. The gray twig color is an identifying characteristic of dwarf yaupon. It is sometimes substituted for Japanese holly or, to a lesser extent, boxwood, because of their similar appearance. However, unlike soft, billowy boxwood, the stems of dwarf yaupon are very stiff and will snap easily. Do not plant it near a basketball goal or other place where its neat mound can be broken.

Dwarf yaupon's natural, rounded form makes it a superb ground cover or foundation plant, since it does not need pruning. It is also easy to shear it into a formal hedge. Because dwarf yaupon is very tolerant of heat, drought, and poor soil, it is a good choice for beach locations. It not only survives in sandy soil but also withstands the withering effects of salt spray. Dwarf yaupon is popular for hot, dry streetside beds and is often planted in the partial shade at the edge of a large, thirsty shade tree.

Holly, Yaupon

Yaupon hollies can serve as small trees in the garden if you prune their lower limbs.

AT A GLANCE
❖

YAUPON HOLLY
Ilex vomitoria

Plant type: evergreen shrub

Landscape use: accent, screen, or specimen

Features: finely textured foliage, profuse red berries

Height: 10 to 15 feet

Width: 10 to 15 feet

Light: full sun to partial shade

Water: low

Pests: none specific

Range: Zones 7 to 9

Remarks: a rugged, fast-growing evergreen that thrives in almost any conditions; excellent seaside planting

Yaupon holly is a durable shrub that will grow to the size of a small tree. Native to the coastal areas of the middle and lower South, it is widely used in Texas and Florida because it tolerates poor soil, heat, and salt spray.

Yaupon grows in an upright, irregular manner to a height and spread of 10 to 15 feet. While its dense growth habit makes yaupon a good screen or hedge, you can also train it into a tree form by removing its lower limbs. As a small tree, it can provide shade in a courtyard.

Yaupon has characteristic gray twigs with small, dark green leaves. In winter, the plant bears a crop of bright red translucent berries that make this its showiest season. However, yaupon's fine texture, evergreen foliage, and sculptural form make it a handsome year-round plant that works well as the focal point of a planting. Yaupon also takes pruning well, making it a handsome espalier.

There are several selections of yaupon holly that grow into narrow trees with a dramatic weeping habit.

These plants are well suited for small gardens and narrow areas where height is needed. Dwarf yaupon is a popular low-growing selection that makes a superb ground cover or foundation plant.

Yaupon will grow in full sun or partial shade, but for best fruiting and dense growth, plant it in full sun. Yaupon will tolerate both acid and alkaline soil as long as it is well drained. At the beach, yaupon's leaves are not bothered by salt spray.

AT A GLANCE

HOSTA
Hosta species

Plant type: perennial

Landscape use: ground cover, seasonal color

Features: lush, textured foliage from summer to fall

Height: 3 to 48 inches

Spread: 3 to 48 inches

Light: shade to partial shade

Water: high to medium

Pests: slugs, snails

Range: Zones 3 to 8

Colors: green, blue green, yellow, variegated

Remarks: splendid foliage color and texture for shade; mass as ground cover or use with ferns in shady settings

Variegated hostas work well as a contrast against plants with solid green leaves.

Hostas will thrive for decades, returning faithfully each spring with a bold rosette of foliage that brings texture and color to even the shadiest areas of a garden. Depending on the type, hostas grow from 3 inches to 4 feet in height. Their foliage color ranges from waxy blue to bright chartreuse or variegated creamy tones. Although not usually grown for their flowers, hostas do produce slender spires of white and lavender lilylike blooms; some, such as those of Royal Standard, are very fragrant and can be used as cut flowers.

These multipurpose perennials are good candidates for accents, borders, small mass plantings, or ground covers. They also make good companions for ferns, caladiums, coleus, impatiens, and other summer shade lovers. Try planting them so that their different sizes and colors form a leafy patchwork design. You will be delighted with the intriguing interplay of light and texture. Hostas with bright gold or chartreuse foliage are especially striking against the deep green shades in a garden. Variegated selections feature green or blue foliage highlighted by rims and swirls of gold, cream, or white.

Hostas do best in filtered morning sun or light dappled by trees. Plant them in a well-drained spot with good soil, and water them frequently. Once planted, you may leave hostas alone, as they rarely need to be divided.

Iris

Bearded iris offer stunning flowers in spring.

AT A GLANCE
❖
IRIS
Iris species

Plant type: perennial

Landscape use: accent, seasonal color

Features: large blooms, grasslike or swordlike foliage

Height: 4 to 48 inches

Spread: 8 to 24 inches

Light: full sun to partial shade

Water: low to high, depending on species

Pests: iris borers

Range: Zones 3 to 10

Colors: almost every color, but especially yellow, blue, bronze, white, purple, multicolored

Remarks: splendid foliage plants and enduring cut flowers; tremendous species variety and many selections

Iris, one of the most widely planted of all the perennials, come in several shapes and sizes. Many, such as Siberian iris, are maintenance free and some, such as Louisiana iris, adapt well to wet soil. All produce classic flowers and handsome foliage that may be as striking as the blooms themselves.

Best known are the bearded iris, which have been extensively hybridized. In mid- to late spring, these plants produce huge blooms with lower petals that sport a goatee of fuzzy hairs. Bearded iris are prized as much for their 8- to 24-inch-tall vertical leaves as for their blooms. They are handsome additions to a flower border, and their foliage is striking when paired with a low-spreading plant. Bearded iris prefer full sun and require well-drained soil. They do best where the soil is moist and fertile.

Louisiana iris are hybrids of several native species. The leaves, which are narrow and upright, grow 3 to 4 feet tall. These iris enjoy moist soil and full sun to partial shade. Siberian iris *(Iris siberica)* are also ideal for wet sites, working well at the edge of a pond or even in water. Siberian iris will grow in dry soil as well, but the soil should be fertile. These plants have grasslike foliage that grows 1 to 3 feet high. Native dwarf crested iris *(Iris cristata)* grow only 4 to 6 inches tall. They carpet the ground in a mass of blue and yellow early-spring blossoms and will spread in shade to form large plantings.

AT A GLANCE

❖

ENGLISH IVY
Hedera helix

Plant type: evergreen vine

Landscape use: ground cover, vine

Features: dark, glossy foliage; vigorous growth both up and out

Height: 1 foot as ground cover, 90 feet as vine

Light: shade to partial shade

Water: medium

Pests: none specific

Range: Zones 4 to 9

Remarks: handsome, stately look; valuable for rapid cover in shady areas; minimal long-term care; can be hard on trees if allowed to climb for many years; confinement can be a challenge

English ivy forms a uniform, low-maintenance ground cover for the entrance to this home.

English ivy is noteworthy for its vigorous growth that is both tenacious and long lived, particularly in deep shade. While the plant is a true climbing vine, adhering to surfaces by means of tiny modified roots along the stems, most gardeners plant it as a ground cover. English ivy tolerates a wide range of sun and soil conditions and, once established, grows rapidly to create a seemingly solid cover no more than 1 foot high. If allowed to climb, it will ascend to 90 feet.

The new leaves are a bright, lustrous green and typically have three to five lobes. They show a whitish coloration in the veins and are particularly vivid against the darker backdrop of the older foliage. Mature English ivy has a rounded leaf and a more upright, shrubby habit. The greenish white flowers of a mature plant are borne in flat-topped clusters suspended from the stems.

English ivy is very popular as a ground cover in the deep shade under trees. However, you must prevent it from climbing up tree trunks by trimming shoots that begin to appear in spring. English ivy is a good choice to train up brick columns, walls, or fences, but because it tends to stick to surfaces, it can loosen old mortar or remove stucco if pulled away. You can keep it low maintenance by edging once or twice a year.

Plant English ivy in shade in the South. Farther north, it can take more sun. Ivy will grow in most soils if it is well drained, but for best growth provide rich, fertile soil.

Leucothoe, Florida

Florida leucothoe has an elegant arching form.

Florida leucothoe has an upright, weeping form that is elegant and graceful. It grows to a height of 8 to 12 feet and eventually will spread 4 to 6 feet wide. An individual plant is composed of many sprays of upright stems that fan skyward and then arch gracefully back to earth. The foliage appears to cascade from the top of the plant to the ground.

The evergreen leaves, which are a glossy medium green, are arranged along the length of the stems and grow 3 to 5 inches long. The new growth has a slightly reddish tint when it emerges from the tips of the branches in early spring. By mid-May, profuse clusters of tiny bell-shaped flowers appear where the leaves join the stems. The flowers remain suspended on the plant, draped like pearls.

Because of its graceful arching stems, Florida leucothoe makes a striking specimen plant in a border. A mass planting of the shrub will create a loose screen. Its glossy evergreen foliage is popular for flower arranging. Although narrow at the base, the plant needs at least 6 feet to cascade gracefully. It makes a soft addition to a foundation planting or a shrub border.

Be sure to keep young plants watered, as they are very sensitive to drought until the roots are well established; this may take two years. Once established, leucothoe needs little care, but it must have moist, well-drained soil. It prefers partial shade, making this shrub a good companion to rhododendron.

AT A GLANCE

LIGUSTRUM
Ligustrum japonicum

Plant type: evergreen shrub

Landscape use: accent, mass or screen planting

Features: glossy evergreen foliage, sculptural form, white flower spikes, profuse blue berries

Height: 6 to 18 feet

Width: 6 to 8 feet

Light: full sun

Water: medium

Pests: whiteflies

Range: Zones 7 to 10

Remarks: a fast-growing shrub with many uses; prune lower limbs to create a stately evergreen courtyard "tree"; use at 6- to 8-foot intervals for a screen planting

Remove ligustrum's lower limbs to create a small tree.

Ligustrum is an inexpensive, fast-growing, and long-lived evergreen. An excellent long-term garden value, ligustrum is undaunted by heat or poor soil. The plant has an upright, rounded form and is covered with 1½- to 4-inch-long dark green leaves that retain their color all year. In late spring and early summer, large panicles of tiny white flowers appear on the tips of the branches and then mature into small blue fruits that last through winter.

Also called Japanese privet, this shrub will grow quickly to 10 to 12 feet. It may reach 18 feet tall in tropical climates, where it is often trained into a small tree. The plant has a sculptural branch structure and a textured gray-brown bark.

Ligustrum's ultimate size is the most important factor to consider in determining its landscape use. Left unpruned, ligustrum can serve as a free-form screen or provide a backdrop for more ornamental flowering shrubs. However, many gardeners prune the shrub to create a tall formal hedge. By removing ligustrum's lower branches, you can create a small evergreen tree. These tree-form plants are popular accents in beds of ground cover.

Ligustrum transplants easily and tolerates difficult growing conditions. Because it withstands severe heat, it is ideal for hot, sunny areas with reflected heat and light. Whiteflies may occasionally bother ligustrum, but the plants seem to tolerate them well.

Liriope

Liriope makes a thick ground cover that serves as a good visual substitute for grass.

AT A GLANCE
❖
LIRIOPE
Liriope species

Plant type: evergreen ground cover

Landscape use: ground cover, seasonal color

Features: grasslike foliage, spikes of summer flowers, absolute dependability

Height: 8 to 18 inches

Light: full sun to shade

Water: low to high

Pests: none specific

Range: Zones 4 to 9

Remarks: a workhorse, particularly *Liriope spicata,* which spreads underground; tolerates varying soil and light conditions

Liriope is perhaps the most popular ground cover in the South, lining countless flower borders, natural areas, and entryways. Liriope (rhymes with calliope) is virtually indestructible. It is so adaptable to various conditions and so resilient that it seems to have only one horticultural requirement to live— it must be planted.

The hallmark of liriope is its grasslike foliage. Its leaves vary in width from ¼ to ½ inch and may be between 8 inches and nearly 2 feet in length, depending on the selection. The foliage is typically medium to dark green in summer with some yellowing during winter. The variegated selections need more sun than solid green types to bring out their brightest color.

Liriope's clumps of grassy foliage grow at a moderate rate each year. New growth appears from the center of each clump. Creeping lilyturf (*Liriope spicata*) spreads by underground stems to rapidly cover an area.

Liriope is so valued for its foliage that the pretty summer flowers are often overlooked. Blooms are carried on tall spikes and range in color from white to purple.

A classic ground cover for sun or shade, you can use liriope to cover a slope, border a walk, edge a bed, encircle a lawn, or provide a grasslike effect under trees.

Plant liriope in almost any soil. It will tolerate dry and wet conditions. Liriope will grow in sun or shade, but it is often more lush in shade.

To keep liriope looking fresh, mow it in late winter to remove leaves that may be yellow or burned by cold.

Madagascar Periwinkle

Madagascar periwinkle is forgiving enough to grow in pots, where a forgotten watering might permanently damage more sensitive plants.

Madagascar periwinkle (also called vinca) thrives in the heat of midsummer, producing blooms continuously until frost browns the foliage. The blossoms may be white, pink, rose, lavender, or bright red, often splashed with a red, pink, or yellow center.

This rugged, drought-tolerant plant grows in a low, spreading fashion, making it well suited for the foreground of a flower border or for a large mass planting. It is also effective spilling over the edge of containers, in-ground planters, and window boxes. Madagascar periwinkle is salt tolerant and is therefore an ideal choice for gardens near the beach. Plants will often reseed, so you may see volunteer seedlings in flower beds each year.

In the spring, set out transplants rather than sowing seeds. Water about once a week for two to three weeks until plants are established. Then water only if plants begin to wilt. Madagascar periwinkle does not respond well to a lot of water and fertilizer; if it becomes too wet, it may rot. These plants like poor, slightly dry soil, hot sun, and little attention.

Magnolia, Sweet Bay

Sweet bay magnolia is a graceful native tree that prefers a rich, moist soil.

AT A GLANCE
❖
SWEET BAY MAGNOLIA
Magnolia virginiana

Plant type: deciduous tree; evergreen in southern part of range

Landscape use: accent, foundation or screen planting

Features: glossy semievergreen foliage, sweet-scented early summer flowers, upright form

Height: 20 to 60 feet, tallest in southern part of range

Spread: 15 to 20 feet

Light: full sun to partial shade

Water: high to medium

Pests: none specific

Range: Zones 5 to 9

Remarks: native to stream banks and swampy sites; excellent, trouble-free small tree; a beautiful multitrunked specimen

Sweet bay magnolia is a tough plant from the Southern wetlands that is developing a reputation as a worthy ornamental tree. Its distinguishing trait is deep green foliage with a contrasting silvery underside. The slightest breeze moving the leaves causes the tree to shimmer. Although evergreen in the coastal and lower South, sweet bay magnolia will lose its foliage from the middle South northward. However, some selections, such as Henry Hicks, remain evergreen through Zone 5.

In its native habitat, sweet bay magnolia may grow to 60 feet, but in residential areas it will generally stay much smaller, reaching just 10 to 30 feet high.

In late spring or early summer, this tree is covered with 2- to 3-inch-wide creamy white blossoms that perfume the garden with a lemony scent. The flowers mature into handsome seedpods filled with red seeds.

Use sweet bay magnolia as an accent plant or as a small shade tree for a patio or a courtyard. The multitrunked form is especially effective when used as a screen planting, particularly in the southern portion of its range, where it is evergreen.

Sweet bay magnolia prefers highly organic, moist soil. This plant also likes full sun but will do well in partial shade. In the northern portions of its range, it should be protected from cold winter winds.

AT A GLANCE

LEATHERLEAF MAHONIA
Mahonia bealei

Plant type: evergreen shrub

Landscape use: accent, foundation planting

Features: sculptural form, yellow flowers, purplish blue fruit

Height: 6 to 10 feet

Width: 6 to 8 feet

Light: partial to full shade

Water: medium

Pests: none specific

Range: Zones 6 to 9

Remarks: a splendid accent plant with year-round interest; riveting form commands attention; good in foundations for visual punctuation; easily transplanted

Leatherleaf mahonia has a sculptural form reminiscent of a tropical fern.

Leatherleaf mahonia is the largest and most durable of the mahonias. A full-grown specimen has a cluster of upright canes that may reach 6 to 10 feet with a spread of 6 to 8 feet. The individual canes are crowned with compound leaves that have 9 to 13 holly-like leaflets that are held nearly parallel to the ground. The glossy blue-green leaflets are 3 to 5 inches long with several spines and are paired along the stems.

Spikes of bright yellow fragrant flowers form at the tops of the stems in late winter or early spring. The flowers mature to clusters of purplish blue berries that seem to have a powdery coating and that linger on the plant until consumed by birds.

Entry courtyards are excellent locations for the line and form of leatherleaf mahonia. Consider using it in front of a stone wall or a wooden fence, or plant a single specimen by a pool. You can use it in a bed or to punctuate a mass of ground cover or the rounded form and softer foliage of azaleas. Try planting it in clusters of three to create a small grove in a corner of a foundation planting. It also works nicely at the edge of a deck as an evergreen screen.

Leatherleaf mahonia grows best in light shade and prefers moist, well-drained soil. Although it cannot take full sun, early morning sun encourages blooming. The shrub will tolerate deep shade but will grow more slowly and produce fewer flowers.

Maple, Red

Red maple glows with brilliant leaves in autumn.

AT A GLANCE
❖
RED MAPLE
Acer rubrum

Plant type: deciduous tree

Landscape use: shade tree

Features: splendid color, rapid growth, handsome shade

Height: 40 to 60 feet

Spread: 40 to 60 feet

Light: full sun

Water: high to medium

Pests: aphids

Range: Zones 3 to 9

Remarks: a shade tree tolerant of many soil conditions; very reliable; selections Autumn Flame, October Glory, and Red Sunset are best for fall color

This popular shade tree gets its name from the showy bright flowers it brings to the waning winter landscape. The blooms, in clusters of as many as 20, are delicately suspended on long red stalks. The flowers mature into the characteristic maple "wings," or **samaras,** which also are bright red, extending the color at least an extra week in late winter.

This fast-growing, medium-sized tree grows to 40 to 60 feet high with an equal spread and is tolerant of a wide range of soil conditions. The 2- to 4-inch-long leaves, with their characteristic three lobes, are deep green with a slightly lighter underside. In fall, the leaves turn brilliant red for a glorious show. In winter, red maple unveils its distinctive smooth, silver-gray bark.

Red maple can be used in a variety of locations. It works well in a row as a formal shade planting, in a drift along one side of the garden, or in a garden border. It is as much at home along a driveway as it is at the edge of existing woods, or even when used as a free-standing specimen.

On a treeless lot, red maple can serve as the primary shade tree for the house. Plant it on the south or southwest side of the house, at least 20 feet from the structure. Red maple casts a light shade that permits lawn grasses to grow right up to the trunk. Watch out for its vigorous root system; do not plant this tree where it will interfere with septic systems.

AT A GLANCE

SUGAR MAPLE
Acer saccharum

Plant type: deciduous tree

Landscape use: shade tree

Features: steady growth, superb form, adaptability, radiant fall color, longevity

Height: 60 to 80 feet, sometimes 100 feet

Spread: 40 to 50 feet

Light: full sun

Water: medium

Pests: none specific

Range: Zones 4 to 7

Remarks: widely grown, excellent all-around tree; slow growing but worth the wait; upright, rounded form

At maturity, sugar maples will tower over homes.

Sugar maple, with its brilliant fall color, is one of the most widely planted shade trees. Its fall show, with a color range of bright yellow to blaze orange, is the best of the native maples. The older trees develop bark that is coarse, rugged, and slightly shaggy, somewhat like that of white oak.

Sugar maple makes an ideal primary shade tree. It will grow slowly to 80 feet with a 40- to 50-foot oval-shaped crown. Large trees will create a deep shade, making it difficult to establish and maintain a good dense turf beneath them.

Be sure to use mulch or ground cover around the base of the tree, where surface roots make mowing difficult. Its uniform, lollipop shape lends itself to straightforward landscape designs; use sugar maples as street trees, or pair them on opposite sides of a sidewalk if there is enough distance between them to allow roots to grow.

Sugar maple needs rich, loose, well-drained soil for best growth. It does not like heavy, compacted soil. This tree may show signs of heat stress in the South by developing scorched or brown leaves. Legacy, Green Mountain, and Gold Spire are three selections that are relatively tolerant of Southern conditions. The native Southern sugar maple (*Acer barbatum*) is similar to sugar maple, only smaller. In the warmer Zones 8 and 9, it is a good substitute for sugar maple.

Mondo Grass

Tufts of mondo grass create the first layer of this colorful sweep. These tufts will spread to form a solid mat.

Mondo grass brings a refinement to shady garden settings that is unequaled by other ground covers. Its 3- to 8-inch-long leaves create a carpet that appears to be a lush and tender lawn. Yet mondo grass is a tough, resilient evergreen plant that maintains a deep color throughout the year, with the exception of some winter browning at the tips of the leaves.

Like liriope, mondo grass expands into a gradually widening clump, eventually growing to a maximum width of 6 inches. To encourage uniform growth, divide its larger clumps into smaller sprigs. Then plant these sprigs at 2- to 3-inch intervals throughout a bed that has been premulched with pulverized pine bark. The initial planting is the only intensive work required for this ground cover. After planting, this carefree evergreen can exist for many years without any attention or thinning.

Use mondo grass in shady areas where you want a ground cover with a grasslike texture.

The dwarf selection Nana is a good filler between stepping stones or in a pot.

Mondo grass will grow in partial to deep shade. It does not like full sun. Although this ground cover tolerates both wet and dry conditions, a hot, dry summer followed by an unusually cold winter can result in cold damage or even winter kill. To prevent this, be sure to water during extended drought.

AT A GLANCE

NANDINA
Nandina domestica

Plant type: evergreen shrub

Landscape use: accent, foundation planting

Features: delicate foliage texture and twiggy form, white summer flowers, profuse winter berries

Height: 1½ to 8 feet

Width: 3 to 4 feet

Light: full sun to shade

Water: medium

Pests: none specific

Range: Zones 6 to 9

Remarks: durable evergreen with fine texture; useful in foundation plantings or as an accent in borders

Nandina is a good choice for tight spaces since it grows up, not out, and is easy to prune.

Nandina's fine-textured foliage belies its reputation as a durable, adaptable evergreen. It grows at a moderate rate to 8 feet tall but rarely gets wider than 4 feet. The plant's form is upright and stemmy, a collection of woody canes sporting finely divided compound leaves.

In late spring, the canes produce large panicles of small white flowers. The flowers mature into green ¼-inch-round fruit that hang in 8-inch-long clusters. The fruit turn brilliant red by early fall and remain on the shrub through winter.

This plant is ideal for problem areas in sun or shade, especially small, confined spaces. Nandina's fine texture contrasts handsomely with stacked stone, clapboard siding, and wood fencing.

Dwarf selections 1 to 2 feet tall, such as Harbour Dwarf, make good ground covers. Others, such as Gulf Stream, are moderately tall, reaching about 4 feet. Many selections grow to a different height, so be sure to check the label when you shop.

Like most plants, nandina grows best in fertile, well-drained soil. However, once established, it is very drought tolerant. Avoid pruning it other than to thin it by removing the oldest, longest canes. For a fuller plant, cut a few canes at ground level; then cut more in one-third increments. Nandina takes full sun and may defoliate in northern limits of its range.

Oak, Live

AT A GLANCE

LIVE OAK
Quercus virginiana

Plant type: evergreen tree

Landscape use: accent, shade tree

Features: broad, spreading crown casts dark, dappled shade; sculptural form

Height: 40 to 80 feet

Spread: 60 to 100 feet

Light: full sun

Water: medium

Pests: none specific

Range: Zones 8 to 10

Remarks: attains its classic form in coastal humidity, will also grow in the Southwest; plant as a specimen or a grove; uncommon strength and durability

A signature tree of the deep South, live oak stretches its heavy limbs in a characteristic spread.

Although live oak grows quickly when young, it takes considerable time to achieve its celebrated shape. In humid, rainy locations, the tree obtains its characteristic form: a short, massive trunk with huge, sprawling main limbs, the lowest of which sweep the ground.

The leaves of live oak are 2 to 4 inches long and ½ to 2 inches wide. During the growing season, they have a smooth texture and are shiny black green. Live oak is considered "evergreen" because the leaves remain on the tree until new spring growth replaces them over a period of weeks in spring. Because of this foliage pattern, live oak casts a deep mottled shade all year.

Live oak is primarily a shade tree, and one specimen is enough to shade a small backyard. Give the tree room to spread by planting in the open lawn (this will also provide the full sun it needs). As the tree matures, casting a deeper shade, you may need to replace the grass underneath with ground cover.

Since it is quite tolerant of heat and salt spray, live oak is a good choice for coastal locations. In arid climates, young live oaks should be grouped close together so that they reach for light; the leaning trunks will provide shade within the landscape.

Plant live oak in well-drained soil. Although tolerant of soil that is occasionally soggy, live oak will not grow in soil that is constantly wet.

AT A GLANCE

❖

OLEANDER
Nerium oleander

Plant type: evergreen shrub

Landscape use: accent, mass or screen planting

Features: profuse flowers, slender evergreen foliage, tolerant of salt spray and heat

Height: 6 to 12 feet

Width: 6 to 12 feet

Light: full sun

Water: medium

Pests: scales, mealybugs, oleander caterpillars

Range: Zones 8 to 10

Remarks: makes a handsome informal screen or accent; all parts of the plant are poisonous

The bright flowers of oleander are only one of its many attributes.

In the deep coastal South, oleander puts on a flowering show that lasts almost all summer long. It ignores the heat, drought, and salt spray and is high on the list of tough, durable evergreens.

The shrub grows at a moderate-to-rapid rate to a mature size of 6 to 12 feet high and wide. Cold temperatures may kill part of the plant in the northern part of its range; however, it recovers quickly from the roots. The form is upright and rounded but can be erratic, since multiple stems originate from the ground. New shoots often carry leaves in whorls at the ends of the branches.

The narrow, gray green leathery leaves are 3 to 5 inches long and taper to a point. Fragrant 1-inch-wide flowers appear in clusters on new growth as early as late June and continue into midfall. The flowers may be single or double and vary in color from white and salmon to pink and red.

Oleander berries, foliage, and flowers are poisonous, so beware of using the plant in areas where pets or small children might ingest a part of the plant. Never burn the wood from oleander, as the smoke is also poisonous.

In spite of its poison, oleander is popular in Florida and the coastal South. You can use it singly or in a group to provide a lovely evergreen screen. If you live north of oleander's range, you can grow the shrub outside in a pot in summer and then bring the plant indoors for winter.

Oleander grows best in full sun and rich, moist, well-drained soil.

Pachysandra, Japanese

Pachysandra is one of the most luxurious of the shade-loving ground covers.

AT A GLANCE
❖
JAPANESE PACHYSANDRA
Pachysandra terminalis

Plant type: evergreen ground cover
Landscape use: ground cover
Features: plush, dressy appearance
Height: 6 to 12 inches
Light: partial to full shade
Water: medium
Pests: none specific
Range: Zones 3 to 8
Remarks: handsome ground cover; does well planted over tree roots; spreads rapidly in soft, fertile topsoil; discolors with sun

Japanese pachysandra is a hardy, durable, dressy ground cover that thrives in partial shade or full shade. It grows at a deliberate rate, but once it is established, the plant becomes a thick tangle of tender foliage and stems that inhibits weeds.

Pachysandra grows to a mature height of 6 to 12 inches. The leaves, which are 2 to 4 inches long and ½ to 1½ inches wide, are held at the top of the upright stems in a whorled fashion. The new growth emerges an appealing light green at the top of the stems and turns a lustrous dark green as it matures. In early spring, pachysandra sends up a 1- to 2-inch-long flower stalk vertically from the stem end in the center of the leaves.

Use Japanese pachysandra as a permanent ground cover in the shade under trees or on the north side of a house. Take advantage of its tendency to spread by letting it cover a large area where grass cannot grow well.

Pachysandra prefers a rich, moist soil and partial shade. You should fertilize every year with a product that contains iron. This will help the foliage develop a deep green color. To speed growth, encourage rooting by mulching with pulverized pine bark. Pour the mulch directly in the bed; the new year's growth will easily root. If the evergreen leaves are browned by winter cold, simply snip off the stems and new leaves will appear.

AT A GLANCE

❖

PANSY
Viola x *wittrockiana*

Plant type: annual

Landscape use: color for the front of flower beds and for pots and window boxes; mixes well with spring bulbs

Features: bright color for fall, winter, and spring

Height: 4 to 8 inches

Width: 8 inches

Light: full sun

Water: medium

Pests: slugs

Range: Zones 3 to 10

Colors: white, orange, yellow, rose, blue, wine, purple

Remarks: one of the most cold-hardy annuals; will tolerate temperatures in the 20s or lower without damage

Pansies bring brilliant color to a garden throughout the fall, winter, and early spring.

Pansies have become the standard cool-weather annual for bringing color to flower beds in fall, winter, and early spring. Their bright flowers come in many shades and may measure from 1½ to 4 inches in diameter, depending on the selection. Some types have cheery markings called "faces," while others are solid in color. Landscape-type pansies, such as Crystal Bowl and Maxim, produce many small flowers. Although large-flowered types, such as Majestic Giants, do not cover themselves with blossoms, their big blooms are popular for cutting.

Pansies are low growing, making them an ideal plant for the front of a flower border or for containers. They are also good companions to early-spring bulbs, such as daffodils and Dutch iris. Some selections emit a gentle fragrance.

In the South, it is best to plant pansies in fall; they will bloom longer and more prolifically than those planted in late winter or spring. Fall-planted pansies sit through cold spells without blooming and then begin to flower when the temperature reaches the 50s. The plants form neat mounds of foliage at first but need trimming back as they grow, especially in spring.

Pansies respond well to rich soil and fertilizer. Be sure to plant them in enriched, well-amended soil, and give them plenty of water during dry fall weather.

Periwinkle

Periwinkle covers the ground with a neat, dense mat of intertwining vines.

Periwinkle continually proves itself as one of the most versatile ground cover vines to flourish in either partial sun or shade. It quickly grows into a mat of glossy evergreen foliage that is dense enough to suppress weeds. Its tenacious root system can anchor the soil on a sloping site and help reduce soil erosion.

For all its usefulness, many gardeners choose periwinkle for the fine texture it adds to the garden. The plant features ½- to 1½-inch dark, glossy green leaves that are paired on the stems. These stems emerge from a central clump to spread quickly in all directions across the ground. When the stems touch the soil, they easily take root, extending periwinkle's coverage in the bed.

In late March or early April, the vines become covered with 1-inch-wide lilac blue flowers that stand up above the foliage. Because of its stemmy, vinelike shoots, it is easy to dig through periwinkle to plant daffodils.

Their yellow blooms make a good companion to periwinkle's blue blossoms.

A related plant *Vinca major* has larger leaves and grows to 18 inches tall. It is better adapted to sun than *Vinca minor*.

Plant periwinkle in rich, moist soil. Be sure to provide shade, as this ground cover will struggle in full sun.

Loblolly pine's filtered light allows most plants to receive enough sun for growth.

Loblolly pine is a fast-growing shade tree that is native to the South. While it will grow to 40 or 50 feet or more in a landscape setting, it can quickly reach 100 feet in the wild.

As with other pine trees, loblolly pines are pyramidal when young, developing a more rounded crown as they mature. Their soft needles are often 8 inches long and grow in bundles of three. The trees have a light green cast through most of the year and produce cones that may remain on the tree for many years.

Inexpensive and reliable, loblolly pine is a good choice for quick shade. It is suitable for naturalizing since it adapts easily to many types of soil.

For the first 10 to 15 years of growth, this tree retains branches as close to the ground as 4 feet, making a group of trees a highly effective evergreen screen. Try planting three to five pines together as an open-lawn feature. Mowing beneath them is easy while they are young, and they will self-mulch when mature.

White pine *(Pinus strobus)* is a good alternative to loblolly pine in the upper South. In the landscape, white pine is finicky about location. It must have cool temperatures and prefers consistently moist, but well-drained, soil. Native trees may be found in dry, rocky areas, while nursery-grown trees prefer conditions that are less harsh.

Pittosporum

Gray-green foliage makes Wheeler's Dwarf one of the most popular pittosporum selections.

Japanese pittosporum is well known for its crisp, dense foliage. These shrubs are invariably neat plants that do not require pruning. They grow slowly and steadily, attaining a mature height of 3 to 10 feet.

Pittosporum's thick evergreen leaves are whorled at the ends of the branches and densely cover the plant. The 3-inch-long leaves are leathery and rounded at the tip and tend to curl under along the sides. The shrub's tiny white to pale yellow flowers are inconspicuous but quite fragrant in late spring.

Pittosporum's mound of foliage makes it an effective privacy planting or screen. If you have larger, older plants, you can limb them up as tree-form specimens. Use pittosporum as an anchor plant in the corner of a walled garden.

Wheeler's Dwarf pittosporum, which grows to about 4 feet tall, is an excellent foundation plant since it requires no pruning to control size and yet adds enough dimension and texture to fill a garden space with interest. Its light gray-green leaves are a good contrast to darker green foliage. Wheeler's Dwarf is less cold hardy than other selections so plant it only in protected locations in the northern reaches of its range.

Pittosporum prefers full sun but will do well in shade. Be sure to provide good drainage. This shrub is tough enough to withstand the heat of full sun and reflected sunlight, as well as salt spray. Protect it from temperatures below 25 degrees.

AT A GLANCE

REDBUD
Cercis canadensis

Plant type: deciduous tree

Landscape use: accent

Features: excellent form, early magenta flowers

Height: 20 to 30 feet

Spread: 25 to 35 feet

Light: full sun to partial shade

Water: medium to low

Pests: canker

Range: Zones 4 to 9

Remarks: an outstanding native tree tolerant of heat and many types of soil; upright spreading form makes it useful as a patio tree; attractive planted at the edge of a natural area

The durable native redbud is one of the first trees to bloom in the spring.

Redbud is a versatile small tree best known for its bright magenta flowers. The tiny pea-shaped blooms sprout directly from the smooth gray bark of the stems and branches and from the knotty older portions of the trunk. The rosy purple buds open into full blooms and fade out before the dogwoods open. The flowers vary from pink to lavender or rose, but the most vivid trees have magenta blooms. Forest Pansy is a selection with dark magenta flowers and bright reddish purple foliage.

Heart-shaped leaves follow the blooms and may grow as wide as 5 inches across. In fall, the foliage changes from light green to vivid butter yellow. A redbud will grow about 2 feet per year, reaching a mature height of 20 to 30 feet.

You can plant this versatile tree singly in a garden or in an open lawn beneath shade trees. Or use it in groupings, in a grove that mimics its natural growth in the woods. In spring, redbud makes a colorful, rustic accent beside a weathered building, and the gray bark is striking in front of a stucco, brick, or wooden wall.

This tree endures heat, drought, and a variety of soil types, making it one of the most adaptable and reliable small trees. The only maintenance drawback is the seedpods, which drop to the ground and must be cleaned up. Seedpods produce seedlings, and these must be pulled from beds where they sprout.

Rose-of-Sharon

Typically, Rose-of-Sharon has pink or lavender flowers, but this selection, Diana, has white blooms.

AT A GLANCE
❖
ROSE-OF-SHARON
Hibiscus syriacus

Plant type: deciduous shrub

Landscape use: in shrub border, as specimen or accent plant

Features: upright, treelike growth; continual summer flowers

Height: 8 to 12 feet

Width: 6 to 10 feet

Light: full sun to partial shade

Water: medium

Pests: Japanese beetles

Range: Zones 5 to 9

Remarks: an indestructible, old-fashioned favorite that flowers during the hottest days

When the summer heat seems unbearable, Rose-of-Sharon opens its hibiscus-like flowers even in the hottest locations. This shrub begins flowering as early as May in the deep South and continues blooming through September or later. Its big 4- to 6-inch-wide flowers in shades of lavender, pink, or white open at dawn and close in the evening.

Rose-of-Sharon grows at a moderate rate into a treelike shrub 8 to 12 feet high and about 8 feet wide. The leaves drop in fall, leaving behind a bare-branched winter form. A young plant is full to the bottom, but as it grows, it becomes vase shaped, which makes the shrub appear thin at the base. You can offset this by removing some of the lower branches, training it to tree form, or using it in a bed of midsize evergreen shrubs.

Rose-of-Sharon works well in a shrub border, either alone or combined with other shrubs, such as evergreen barberry, spirea, or forsythia.

You will find shrubs simply labeled Rose-of-Sharon, but there are named selections chosen for their flower color. Aphrodite has a deep rose-pink shell with a red eye. Cedar Lane has white petals with a red center, while Diana has a big, pure white blossom, which remains open at night.

Rose-of-Sharon grows in full sun or partial shade. It prefers moist, well-drained soil but is tolerant of a variety of soils. The only drawback to this shrub is that it will reseed itself; pulling the seedlings can become a chore. However, many of the new selections, such as Diana, do not reseed.

AT A GLANCE
❖
SHOWY SEDUM
Sedum spectabile

Plant type: perennial

Landscape use: seasonal color

Features: thick, fleshy leaves; colorful flowers in early to late fall

Height: 1 to 2 feet

Spread: 1 to 3 feet

Light: full sun to partial shade

Water: low

Pests: none specific

Range: Zones 4 to 9

Colors: pink, red, bronze

Remarks: a curious-looking but long-lived, dependable plant; profuse late-season flowers last until a hard freeze

This showy sedum selection, Autumn Joy, provides a lengthy blooming season of pink to bronze flowers atop fleshy foliage.

Showy sedum is a rugged, durable perennial that looks good even when it is not in bloom. As long as it receives plenty of sun and has good drainage, showy sedum puts on an attractive display, blooming in dry weather and poor soil.

Although it does not bloom until fall, showy sedum emerges in spring with succulent rosettes of leaves that grow into lush mounds of gray-green foliage. By mid-summer, flower buds are formed; these buds resemble beaded tufts and appear atop the pale, fleshy leaves. In fall, buds gradually unfold into starlike clusters of pink, rose, crimson, or copper.

The sturdy, almost shrub-like, form makes showy sedum a good companion to shrubs and other perennials. Plant it with mums, ornamental grasses, coneflowers, asters, and other fall-blooming perennials and annuals. You may also use it to provide textural contrast for finer-leafed shrubs, such as Scotch broom and dwarf yaupon.

Showy sedum does best in full sun but will grow in light shade. However, if you grow these flowers in the shade, you may need to cut them back by about one-third their height in early summer to prevent them from becoming too leggy. The only conditions that showy sedum will not tolerate are deep shade and poor drainage.

Spirea, Reeves

Reeves spirea is a large, fountainlike shrub, so give it plenty of room to show off its graceful form.

AT A GLANCE
❖
REEVES SPIREA
Spiraea cantoniensis

Plant type: deciduous shrub

Landscape use: accent, mass or screen planting

Features: vigorous growth, profuse bouquets of tiny white flowers covering every arching branch

Height: 4 to 5 feet

Width: 4 to 5 feet

Light: full sun to light shade

Water: medium

Pests: none specific

Range: Zones 6 to 9

Remarks: large shrub to be used as a natural screen or in a mixed border; offers substantial long-term reward with little attention

---

Reeves spirea is one of the best of a group of shrubs that are durable, care-free, exquisite in bloom, and graceful year-round. This long-lived deciduous shrub grows rapidly to a height and spread of 4 to 5 feet.

The fine-textured, blue-green leaves of Reeves spirea are 1 to 2½ inches long and less than ¾ inch wide. Fall color is insignificant and the leaves may persist through late fall. In the deep South, this deciduous shrub is sometimes considered evergreen.

In the spring, Reeves spirea is covered with dense bouquetlike clusters of white blossoms along the length of every stem.

These large shrubs work best as billowing masses or natural hedges at the edge of a garden, along a property line, or on a slope. Use Reeves spirea to soften the side of a wall or to screen an undesirable view. The shrub's branch network is so dense that it can serve as an effective screen even in winter. The handsome foliage and arching form make Reeves spirea an excellent backdrop for a perennial border. Or use the shrub as a specimen planting. Be sure to provide plenty of room for it to grow.

Reeves spirea prefers full sun and rich, well-drained soil. However, it will tolerate almost any soil and a fair amount of shade, although it does not bloom as heavily in shade. In full sun, it will develop its characteristic mounding form with arching stems that are weighted down with spring flowers.

118

Star Jasmine, Japanese

JAPANESE STAR JASMINE
Trachelospermum asiaticum

Plant type: evergreen vine

Landscape use: ground cover, vine

Features: glossy, dark green foliage; flowers in spring

Height: 12 to 15 inches as ground cover; 20 feet as vine

Light: full sun to deep shade

Water: low

Pests: none specific

Range: Zones 7 to 9

Remarks: a drought-tolerant ground cover that grows well under trees

Japanese star jasmine will grow in sun or shade.

Japanese star jasmine (also known as Asian star jasmine) is treasured in the deep South as a reliable ground cover for the deepest shade, thriving even under spreading live oaks. Most popular in the coastal South, it is also valued for its indifference to poor soil and ability to tolerate full sun as well as shade.

The vine bears small, deep green, glossy evergreen leaves 1 to 1½ inches long. In winter, plants in the northern reaches of its range develop a red-bronze hue as the leaves are nipped by frost. Vines spread to lengths of 10 to 20 feet, rooting as they grow. They knit and tangle through each other rapidly, forming a mat of leaves 12 to 15 inches high. The vines are easy to maintain. Just shear the top each spring to remove old foliage and encourage branching. Once established, the wiry stems grow together to form a thick cover that competes with weeds.

Use Japanese star jasmine as a ground cover under spreading trees or in sun. It also provides a fine-textured mat when used as a ground cover to tie together shrubs in a foundation planting.

Although most gardeners use it as a ground cover, you can also grow this vine on a wall or trellis. There, it will climb to 20 feet or more, but it will need wire or a thin trellis to wrap around as it climbs.

You can grow Japanese star jasmine in sun to deep shade. Most well-drained soil will support its rapid growth, but it grows best if you mulch with compost or finely ground bark. This gives the vines a good medium in which to root as they spread. When planting, snip the end of each stem to encourage branching.

Viburnum, Doublefile

Doublefile viburnum is often limbed up into a small tree.

AT A GLANCE

❖

DOUBLEFILE VIBURNUM
Viburnum plicatum tomentosum

Plant type: deciduous shrub

Landscape use: accent, mass or foundation planting

Features: distinctive horizontal branches, white flowers, abundant fruit, fall color

Height: 5 to 15 feet

Width: 10 to 18 feet

Light: full sun to partial shade

Water: medium

Pests: none specific

Range: Zones 5 to 8

Remarks: underused plant with striking landscape impact; easy to grow; can serve as a small courtyard tree or open-lawn specimen; grows where dogwoods struggle; effective at the edge of natural areas

Doublefile viburnum is a vigorous plant with a spectacular show of flowers and fruit. It grows rapidly to 15 feet tall and 18 feet wide, and its multitrunked form and horizontal branching resemble that of a small tree. The deep green foliage is layered on top of the branches, emphasizing their horizontal structure. The shrub's dark green leaves are deeply veined, giving them a rough-textured look.

The flowers of doublefile viburnum are borne in two parallel rows along each branch in an attractive display. Each bloom contains a group of tiny yellow fertile flowers in the center that later form seeds. A ring of large white flowers surrounds them.

Doublefile viburnum blooms between April and early May; the flowers are followed in July and August by clumps of fruit that turn bright red and gradually change to black. In fall, the plant turns vivid scarlet, putting on a final show before the leaves drop for winter.

Plant doublefile viburnum in an open lawn where its lower branches will reach the ground, or train it as a small tree with room to pass beneath it. Paired with a foundation planting, it softens the vertical line of a house.

Although doublefile viburnum has a shallow root system and needs rich, well-drained soil, it is bothered by few pests. Once established, it will grow rapidly.

AT A GLANCE

❖

WAX BEGONIA
Begonia x *semperflorens-cultorum*

Plant type: annual

Landscape use: seasonal color

Features: long-lived summer color, ground-hugging habit

Height: 6 to 12 inches

Width: 12 to 18 inches

Light: full sun to partial shade

Water: medium

Pests: rot

Range: Zones 4 to 10

Colors: red, pink, white, salmon, bicolored

Remarks: needs rich soil; produces profuse flowers; excellent for edging or containers

Wax begonia does extremely well as an edging.

From early spring until frost, wax begonia creates a mound of long-lasting color that always stays neatly in place. Plants have a tidy habit and small, silky flowers. The blooms may be creamy white, pink, red, salmon, or bicolored. Leaves are green or bronze, depending on the selection; bronze-leafed types are more tolerant of sun.

Growing only 6 to 12 inches tall, wax begonias are excellent for edging walkways and the borders of raised beds. Clusters of three to five plants can bring a splash of color to a shaded or partially sunny bed; however, they are most effective when planted in gently curving lines.

Wax begonias are a good choice for pots and window boxes because they tolerate heat and dry weather. In containers, their delicate flowers are best appreciated when viewed up close. Combine green-leafed selections with ferns, coleus, or caladiums. Bronze-leafed types are striking companions for plants with silver foliage, such as annual dusty miller or perennial artemisia.

Plant wax begonias after the threat of frost is past. They will do best in rich soil that retains moisture but drains well. Poor drainage will encourage rot. Wax begonias thrive under hot, humid conditions and resist drought once established.

Wax Myrtle

AT A GLANCE

❖

WAX MYRTLE
Myrica cerifera

Plant type: evergreen shrub

Landscape use: accent, mass or screen planting

Features: bayberry-scented foliage, rapid growth

Height: 10 to 20 feet

Width: 15 to 20 feet

Light: full sun to partial shade

Water: high to medium, drought tolerant when established

Pests: none specific

Range: Zones 7 to 10

Remarks: free-form, easy to grow, evergreen to semievergreen; ideal for naturalistic screens or tree-form shrubs around patios

Wax myrtle grows large enough to plant as a small tree.

Wax myrtle offers gardeners a winning combination of grace and utility. Its foliage whorls around the branches and is carried on an upturned angle to the stem, giving the shrub a wispy, breezy look. In addition, it adapts easily to different light and soil conditions.

Native from Maryland to Texas and Florida, wax myrtle grows quickly to an average height and spread of 10 to 20 feet. In the lower and coastal South, it will grow to treelike proportions, casting a mottled shade. The shrub's hallmark is its glossy green narrow leaves.

Wax myrtle is most commonly used as a screen or hedge along a property line. It is a natural complement to young pines for screening both high and low views. It also provides a good background for such deciduous plants as oakleaf hydrangea and forsythia. The soft, delicate texture of wax myrtle blends nicely with coarse, broad-leafed evergreens, such as cleyera and pittosporum.

Dwarf selections work well as foundation plantings. The selection Emperor has very narrow leaves that give it a fine texture. The shrub, which grows 8 to 10 feet tall, appears conifer-like from a distance.

Wax myrtle adapts to a wide variety of growing conditions, including full sun, partial shade, dry or soggy soil. In coastal areas, wax myrtle even blocks salt spray, sheltering less salt-tolerant plants. Because it withstands temperature extremes, it works well in parking lots and containers.

AT A GLANCE

❖

NARROWLEAF ZINNIA
Zinnia angustifolia

Plant type: annual

Landscape use: seasonal color

Features: heat tolerant; nonstop blooms

Height: 1 foot

Width: 2 feet

Light: full sun

Water: low to medium

Pests: none specific

Range: Zones 4 to 10

Colors: orange, creamy white

Remarks: useful as a ground cover; profuse
producer of daisylike flowers with fine foliage

Spilling over the edge of a low wall, narrowleaf zinnia appears more like a wildflower than a cultivated annual.

Narrowleaf zinnia looks more like a wildflower than a zinnia. Dependable and heat tolerant, this plant is covered with small orange or white daisylike flowers that last from spring until frost. It grows into a multibranched, creeping plant about 1 foot tall and twice as wide and is covered with fine, slender blue-green leaves.

Narrowleaf zinnia works well in a summer flower border as a low plant for edging. Unlike other zinnias, it is not bothered by mildew. No matter where you plant it, this annual will usually attract butterflies. Its low, creeping habit makes it ideal for massing as a summer ground cover in a sunny bed. It also serves as a nice carpet of color around taller plants, such as Mexican bush sage, and it looks good spilling over a wall or the edge of a container. Narrowleaf zinnia's growth is loose and wildflower-like, making it a good choice for sunny areas of a natural, informal landscape; try it in a border around an informal water feature or even in a vegetable garden to attract bees for pollination.

You can start narrowleaf zinnia from seed or from transplants. It must have a sunny spot and well-drained soil. Water regularly until established. To keep the zinnias blooming, cut the spent blossoms often so that the plant will continue to produce more flowers.

Pest and Disease Control

Most of the plants in this book do not have serious problems with pests. The few insects and diseases most likely to attack are listed below. Remember, the best way to minimize pest problems is to keep your plants healthy by planting properly and following up with good care.

When applying pesticides, always read the label carefully, and apply only according to label directions. Choose the least toxic options, such as horticultural oil and insecticidal soap, first. Contact your county Extension agent for the latest recommendations on products approved by the Environmental Protection Agency.

Pests

Pest	Description/Damage	Control
Aphid (crepe myrtle, daylily, red maple)	tiny, pear-shaped insects appear by hundreds on new growth and flower buds, distorting them	spray at first sign of infestation with strong jet of water or approved insecticide
Canna leaf roller (canna)	caterpillar that rolls itself in new leaves, chewing holes in them	spray at first sign of infestation or pick caterpillar from plant
Iris borer (iris)	caterpillar that burrows through rhizomes, causing leaves to turn yellow, drip sap, and die back; infected plants look ragged at base	clean up old, brown foliage in fall; in spring, spray lower half of plant with approved insecticide
Japanese beetle (rose-of-Sharon)	½-inch-long, metallic green and copper beetles chew on foliage; can strip plants of all leaves	dust foliage with approved insecticide at first sign of infestation; kill beetle grubs that live in lawn with a grub killer
Lacebug (azalea)	flat insects with lacy wings feed on leaves, sucking sap and causing leaves to dry, curl, and fall; deposit tiny black spots of excrement on underside of leaves	spray at first sign of infestation with approved insecticide in spring or summer
Leaf miner (azalea)	tiny caterpillar miners eat through foliage, leaving blisters and serpentine trails or "mines" that disfigure leaves	difficult to control because miners are protected inside plant; apply approved systemic insecticide at first sign of infestation
Mealybug (oleander)	¼-inch-long, soft-bodied insects covered in white, cottonlike waxy threads; suck sap from leaves and stems, causing distorted growth and yellowing	apply approved insecticide at first sign of infestation
Nematode (daylily)	microscopic eel-like pests live in soil and attack roots; plants stop growing or may yellow and die back	no pesticides approved; add plenty of organic matter to soil; water and fertilize to keep plants in top condition
Oleander caterpillar (oleander)	1½-inch-long orange caterpillar with long tufts of black hair chews holes in leaves; can strip entire stems of foliage	apply approved insecticide at first sign of infestation

Pest	Description/Damage	Control
Scale (Burford holly, oleander)	soft- or hard-bodied insects that cling to stems and leaf undersides; appear to be stuck to plant; suck sap, causing leaves to turn yellow	spray at first sign of infestation with approved insecticide; spray in winter and spring with horticultural oil
Slug, Snail (daylily, hosta, pansy)	pests that feed at night, chewing holes in tender foliage; sign of presence is a shiny slime trail	slug baits and traps
Spider mite (daylily, Burford holly)	minute, spiderlike insects feed on buds and undersides of leaves; suck plant sap and cause foliage and buds to turn brown	overhead watering helps knock mites from foliage; spray at first sign of infestation with approved insecticide
Thrip (daylily)	tiny torpedo-shaped insects feed inside flowers; cause blooms to turn brown where they feed	spray at first sign of infestation with approved insecticide
Whitefly (ligustrum)	adults look like tiny white moths on leaf underside; larvae resemble drops of clear wax; distort new growth	spray at first sign of infestation with approved insecticide

Diseases

Diseases	Description/Damage	Control
Canker (redbud)	fungus that infects trees through wounds, causing sunken, oval lesions or cankers that can girdle branches	avoid injuring bark; prune and destroy infected branches
Leaf spot (Indian hawthorn)	fungus can cause spots on leaves; may cause leaves to yellow or drop	remove infected leaves and spray at first sign of infestation with approved fungicide
Powdery mildew (crepe myrtle)	white to gray mildewlike growth appears on leaves; stunts growth	plant resistant selections; spray in spring and fall with approved fungicide if infection causes severe leaf drop
Rot (Madagascar periwinkle, wax begonia)	overwatering or poor drainage can cause roots and crown of annuals and perennials to rot	avoid overwatering; provide good drainage; once rot begins it is difficult to control
Sclerotinia leaf fungus (aucuba)	brown spots appear along leaf margins; serious infection can cause leaf drop	remove affected leaves and branches
Sooty mold (crepe myrtle)	black sootlike fungus that covers leaves; harmless but ugly	spray with horticultural oil to dislodge black fungus; control feeding by aphids, which secrete sugary excrement on which fungus grows

Index

*A*belia, 64
Abelia x *grandiflora. See* Abelia, 64
Acer rubrum. See Red maple, 104
Acer saccharum. See Sugar maple, 105
Agarista populifolia. See Florida
   leucothoe, 98
Alignment, 13
Amaranth, globe, 87
American holly, 90
Aphids, 79, 82, 104, 124
Asian star jasmine. *See* Japanese star
   jasmine, 119
Aucuba, 55, 57, 58, 65
Aucuba japonica. See Aucuba, 65
Azalea, 55, 58
Azalea, gumpo, 66
Azalea x *satsuki Gumpo. See* Gumpo
   azalea, 66

*B*ald cypress, 67
Beach, plants suited for the, 61
Bearded iris, 96
Beds
   flower, 24–25, 42–43
   raised, 56
Beech, 68
Beetles, Japanese, 116, 124
Begonia, wax, 25, 121
Begonia x *semperflorens-cultorum. See*
   Wax begonia, 121
Bermuda grasses, 23, 30
Black-eyed Susan, 18, 69
Borders, 18, 21–22
Borers, iris, 96, 124
Burford holly, 60, 92
Burning bush. *See* Winged euonymus

*C*aladium, 14, 70
Caladium x *hortulanum. See* Caladium, 70
Canker, 115, 125
Canna, 71, 124
Canna leaf rollers, 71, 124
Canna x *generalis. See* Canna, 71
Caterpillars, 71, 109, 124
Catharanthus roseus. See Madagascar
   periwinkle, 101

Cercis canadensis. See Redbud, 115
Chaenomeles species. See Flowering
   quince, 84
Chaste tree, 72
Chinese holly. *See* Burford holly
Chrysanthemum x *superbum. See* Shasta
   daisy, 81
Cleyera, 55, 73
Coleus, 74
Coleus x *hybridus. See* Coleus, 74
Common Bermuda, 23, 30
Common cosmos, 78
Coneflower
   orange, 47, 75
   purple, 76
Containers, 18, 101
Controlled-release fertilizers, 42
Coreopsis, 77
Coreopsis species. See Coreopsis, 77
Cosmos, 78
Cosmos sulphureus. See Klondyke cosmos, 78
Courtyard gardens, 54–55
Crape myrtle. *See* Crepe myrtle
Creeping lilyturf, 100
Crepe myrtle, 55, 60, 79
Cypress, bald, 67

*D*affodil, 80
Daisy, Shasta, 81
Daylily, 82
Deadheading, 18
Design. *See* Landscaping
Diseases, 124–125. *See also* specific
   diseases
Doublefile viburnum, 120
Drainage, 47, 49
Drought-resistant plants, 60
Dwarf crested iris, 96
Dwarf yaupon holly, 36, 55, 60, 61, 93

*E*chinacea purpurea. See* Purple
   coneflower, 76
Edgings, 50
English ivy, 23, 97
Equipment and tools, 36–38
Erosion, 46–47, 48–49

Euonymus, winged, 83
Euonymus alata. See Winged euonymus, 83

*F*agus grandifolia. See* Beech, 68
Fertilizing, 9, 37, 42–44
Florida leucothoe, 55, 58, 98
Flower beds, 24–25
   fertilizing, 42–43
Flowering quince, 84
Forsythia, 85
Forsythia x *intermedia. See* Forsythia, 85
Foster holly, 90–91
Foundation plantings, 45–46
Fungus. *See* Diseases

*G*ardening, low-maintenance. *See*
   Landscaping, low-maintenance
Gardens
   courtyard, 54–55
   entry, 57–58
   formal vs. informal, 16
   hot and dry, 59–60
   passageway, 57
   seaside, 61
   shade, 58–59
   small, 54–56
   townhouse, 55–56
   wetland, 48
Ginkgo, 60, 86
Ginkgo biloba. See Ginkgo, 86
Globe amaranth, 87
Glossy abelia, 64
Goldenrain tree, 60, 88
Goldsturm. *See* Orange coneflower
Gomphrena globosa. See Globe
   amaranth, 87
Grasses, 23, 28–31. *See also* Lawns
   drought-tolerant, 60
Grasses, cool season, 28
   creeping red fescue, 31
   Kentucky bluegrass, 31
   perennial ryegrass, 31
   tall fescue, 31
Grasses, warm-season, 28
   Bahia, 30
   Bermuda, 30

Buffalo grass, 30
centipede, 30
St. Augustine, 30
Zoysia, 30
Ground covers, 23–24, 46
suited for the beach, 61
Gumpo azalea, 66

*H*awthorn, Indian, 55, 61, 89
Hedera helix. See English ivy, 97
Hemerocallis and hybrids. *See*
Daylily, 82
Herbicides, 9, 33
Hibiscus syriacus. See
Rose-of-Sharon, 116
Holly, 90–94
American, 90
Burford, 60, 92
Chinese. *See* Burford
dwarf yaupon, 36, 55, 60, 61, 93
Foster, 90–91
yaupon, 60, 61, 94
Hosta, 95
Hosta species. See Hosta, 95

*I*lex cornuta *Burfordii. See* Burford
holly, 92
Ilex opaca. See American holly, 90
Ilex vomitoria. Nana. *See* Dwarf yaupon
holly, 93
Ilex vomitoria. See Yaupon holly, 94
Ilex x *attenuata* Foster. *See* Foster
holly, 90–91
Indian hawthorn, 55, 61, 89
Insecticides, 124–125
Invasive plants, 21
Iris, 48, 96
Iris borers, 96, 124
Iris species. See Iris, 96
Ivy, English, 23, 97

*J*apanese aucuba, 55, 57, 58, 65
Japanese beetles, 116, 124
Japanese cleyera, 55, 73
Japanese pachysandra, 110
Japanese pittosporum, 55, 61, 114

Japanese privet. *See* Ligustrum
Japanese star jasmine, 119
Jonquil. *See* Daffodil

*K*londyke cosmos, 78
Koelreuteria paniculata. See Goldenrain
tree, 88

*L*acebugs, 66, 124
Lagerstroemia indica and hybrids. *See*
Crepe myrtle, 79
Landscaping, low-maintenance, 6–11
design, 7, 12–19, 26–28, 54–58
plantings, 20–25, 45–46
seasonal tasks, 9–11
solutions, 45–53
special features, 17–19
Lawn mowers, 37, 44, 51
Lawns, 19, 23
design, 26–28
edgings, 50
eroded areas, 52
fertilizing, 43–44
grasses, 23, 28–31
herbicides, 9
mowing, 10, 27, 28, 44, 51
planting, 34
preparing soil for, 33
Leaf miners, 66, 124
Leaf rollers, canna, 71, 124
Leaf spot, 89, 125
Leatherleaf mahonia, 55, 58, 60, 103
Leucothoe, Florida, 55, 58, 98
Ligustrum, 60, 99
Ligustrum japonicum. See Ligustrum, 99
Lilyturf, creeping, 100
Liriope, 4, 19, 100
Liriope species. See Liriope, 100
Live oak, 60, 61, 108
Loblolly pine, 113
Louisiana iris, 48, 96

*M*adagascar periwinkle, 18, 101
Magnolia, sweet bay, 55, 102
Magnolia virginiana. See Sweet bay
magnolia, 102

Mahonia bealei. See Leatherleaf
mahonia, 103
Mahonia, leatherleaf, 55, 58, 60, 103
Maple
red, 104
sugar, 105
Mealybugs, 109, 124
Mildew, powdery, 79, 125
Mites, spider, 82, 92, 125
Mold, sooty, 79, 125
Mondo grass, 8, 52, 63, 106
Moss, 48
Mowers, 37, 44, 51
Mowing, 10, 27, 28, 44, 51
Mulching, 10, 24, 40–41
Myrica cerifera. See Wax myrtle, 122
Myrtle, wax, 60, 61, 122

*N*andina, 55, 58, 60, 107
Nandina domestica. See Nandina, 107
Narcissus species. See Daffodil, 80
Narrowleaf zinnia, 18, 123
Native plants, 18, 20
Nematodes, 82, 124
Nerium oleander. See Oleander, 109

*O*ak, live, 60, 61, 108
Oleander, 60, 61, 109
Oleander caterpillars, 109, 124
Ophiopogon japonicus. See Mondo
grass, 106
Orange coneflower, 47, 75
Ornaments, garden, 56

*P*achysandra, Japanese, 110
Pachysandra terminalis. See Japanese
pachysandra, 110
Pansy, 111
Paths. *See* Walkways
Perianths, 80
Periwinkle, 112
Periwinkle, Madagascar, 18, 101
Pests, 124–125. *See also* specific pests
Pine, loblolly and white, 113
Pinus taeda. See Loblolly pine, 113
Pittosporum, 55, 61, 114

Index

Pittosporum tobira. See Pittosporum, 114
Plant hardiness zone map, 62
Planting, 10, 34–36
Plugs, 34
Pots. *See* Containers
Powdery mildew, 79, 125
Pre-emergence herbicide, 9
Privet, Japanese. *See* Ligustrum
Pruning, 17
Purple coneflower, 76

*Q*uercus virginiana. *See* Live oak, 108
Quince, flowering, 84

*R*ainfall, 15
Raised beds, 56
Raking, 11, 22, 36, 37
Raphiolepis indica. See Indian
    hawthorn, 89
Redbud, 55, 60, 115
Red maple, 104
Reeves spirea, 118
Retaining walls, 47
Rock work, 46–47
Rose-of-Sharon, 116
Rot, 101, 121, 125
Rudbeckia fulgida. See Orange
    coneflower, 75
Rudbeckia hirta. See Black-eyed Susan, 69

*S*alt spray, plants tolerant of, 61
Samaras, 104
Scales, 92, 109, 125
Scapes, 82
Sclerotinia leaf fungus, 65, 125
Screens, 53
Sedum, 117
Sedum spectabile. See Sedum, 117
Seed, 34
Shade, 27
    gardens, 58–59
    shrubs, 58
Shasta daisy, 81
Showy sedum, 117
Shrubs
    drought-tolerant, 60

fertilizing, 42–43
planting, 35–36
preparing soil for, 33–34
pruning, 17
shade, 58
small, 55
spacing, 36
suited for the beach, 61
Siberian iris, 96
Slopes, 27, 46–47
Slugs, 82, 95, 111, 125
Snails, 95, 125
Sod, 34
Soil, 14
    preparing, 32–34
    testing, 33
Sooty mold, 79, 125
Spacing, 22
    shrubs, 36
Spider mites, 82, 92, 125
Spiraea cantoniensis. See Reeves
    spirea, 118
Spirea, Reeves, 118
Sprigs, 34
Star jasmine, Japanese, 119
Structures, garden, 17–18
Sugar maple, 105
Sun, 13, 14, 27
Sweet bay magnolia, 55, 102

*T*axodium distichum. *See* Bald
    cypress, 67
Ternstroemia gymnanthera. See Cleyera, 73
Terracing, 47
Thatch, 44
Thrips, 82, 125
Tickseed. *See* Coreopsis
Tools and equipment, 36–38
Topography, 13
Townhouse gardens, 55–56
Trachelospermum asiaticum. See
    Japanese star jasmine, 119
Trees
    drought-tolerant, 60
    fertilizing, 42–43
    maintenance problems, 51–52

planting, 35
preparing soil for, 33–34
roots above ground, 51
small, 55
suited for the beach, 61

*V*arnish tree. *See* Goldenrain tree
Viburnum, doublefile, 120
Viburnum plicatum tomentosum. See
    Doublefile viburnum, 120
Vinca minor. See Periwinkle, 112
Vinca. *See* Madagascar periwinkle
Viola x *wittrockiana. See* Pansy, 111
Vitex agnus-castus. See Chaste tree, 72
Vitex. *See* Chaste tree

*W*alkways, 17, 19, 52, 57
Walls, retaining, 47
Water erosion, 48–49
Watering, 11, 39–40
Wax begonia, 25, 121
Wax myrtle, 60, 61, 122
Weeding, 9
Wetland gardens, 48
Wet sites, 47–48
Whiteflies, 99, 125
White pine, 113
Wind erosion, 49
Winged euonymus, 83

*Y*aupon holly, 60, 61, 94
Yaupon holly, dwarf, 35, 55, 60, 61, 93

*Z*innia angustifolia. *See* Narrowleaf
    zinnia, 123
Zinnia, narrowleaf, 18, 123
Zone map, plant hardiness, 62

*S*pecial *T*hanks

All-America Selections, photograph, 71

Jim Bathie, photograph, 98

Southern Progress Corporation Library Staff